DATE DUE			

PSYCHOLOGY

THE BEHAVIORAL AND SOCIAL SCIENCES SURVEY
Psychology Panel

Kenneth E. Clark, *Chairman*
University of Rochester

George A. Miller, *Co-Chairman*
The Rockefeller University

Launor Carter
Systems Development Corporation

Wayne R. Holtzman
University of Texas

Neal E. Miller
The Rockefeller University

Carl Pfaffmann
The Rockefeller University

Richard L. Solomon
University of Pennsylvania

Eliot Stellar
University of Pennsylvania

John W. Thibaut
University of North Carolina

Robert D. Wirt
University of Minnesota

PSYCHOLOGY

Edited by
Kenneth E. Clark and George A. Miller

A SPECTRUM BOOK

Prentice-Hall, Inc., *Englewood Cliffs, N. J.*

150
B39p
75495
Sept. 1971

Current printing (last number):
10 9 8 7 6 5 4 3 2 1

Prentice-Hall International, Inc. (*London*)
Prentice-Hall of Australia, Pty. Ltd. (*Sydney*)
Prentice-Hall of Canada, Ltd. (*Toronto*)
Prentice-Hall of India Private Limited (*New Delhi*)
Prentice-Hall of Japan, Inc. (*Tokyo*)

FOREWORD

This book is one of a series prepared in connection with the Survey of the Behavioral and Social Sciences conducted between 1967 and 1969 under the auspices of the Committee on Science and Public Policy of the National Academy of Sciences and the Problems and Policy Committee of the Social Science Research Council.

The Survey provides a comprehensive review and appraisal of these rapidly expanding fields of knowledge, and constitutes a basis for an informed, effective national policy to strengthen and develop these fields even further.

The reports in the Survey, each the work of a panel of scholars, include studies of anthropology, economics, geography, history as a social science, political science, psychology, psychiatry as a behavioral science, sociology, and the social science aspects of statistics, mathematics and computation. A general volume, *The Behavioral and Social Sciences: Outlook and Needs* (Englewood Cliffs, N.J.: Prentice-Hall, 1969), discusses relations among the disciplines, broad questions of utilization of the social sciences by society, and makes specific recommendations for public and university policy.

While close communication among all concerned has been the rule, the individual panel reports are the responsibility of the panels producing them. They have not been formally reviewed or approved by the Central Planning Committee or by the sponsoring organizations. They were reviewed at an earlier stage by representatives of the National Academy of Sciences and the Social Science Research Council.

Much of the data on the behavioral and social sciences in universities used in these reports comes from a 1968 questionnaire survey,

v

conducted by the Survey Committee, of universities offering the PhD in one of these fields. Questionnaires were filled out by PhD-granting departments (referred to as the Departmental Questionnaire); by selected professional schools (referred to as the Professional School Questionnaire); by computation centers (referred to as the Computation Center Questionnaire); by university financial offices (referred to as the Administration Questionnaire); and by research institutes, centers, laboratories and museums engaged in research in the behavioral and social sciences (referred to as the Institute Questionnaire). Further information concerning this questionnaire survey is provided in the appendix to the general report of the Central Planning Committee, mentioned above.

Also included in the appendix of the report of Central Planning Committee is a discussion of the method of degree projection used in these reports, as well as some alternative methods.

**THE BEHAVIORAL AND SOCIAL SCIENCES
SURVEY COMMITTEE
CENTRAL PLANNING COMMITTEE**

Ernest R. Hilgard, *Stanford University*, CHAIRMAN
Henry W. Riecken, *Social Science Research Council*,
    CO-CHAIRMAN
Kenneth E. Clark, *University of Rochester*
James A. Davis, *Dartmouth College*
Fred R. Eggan, *The University of Chicago*
Heinz Eulau, *Stanford University*
Charles A. Ferguson, *Stanford University*
John L. Fischer, *Tulane University of Louisiana*
David A. Hamburg, *Stanford University*
Carl Kaysen, *Institute for Advanced Study*
William H. Kruskal, *The University of Chicago*
David S. Landes, *Harvard University*
James G. March, *University of California, Irvine*
George A. Miller, *The Rockefeller University*
Carl Pfaffmann, *The Rockefeller University*
Neil J. Smelser, *University of California, Berkeley*
Allan H. Smith, *Washington State University*
Robert M. Solow, *Massachusetts Institute of Technology*
Edward Taaffe, *The Ohio State University*
Charles Tilly, *The University of Michigan*
Stephen Viederman, *National Academy of Sciences*,
    EXECUTIVE OFFICER

CONTENTS

vii

PSYCHOLOGY

PREFACE

Our purpose in the following pages is to convey to the reader information about psychology, to show the variety of activities in which psychologists are engaged, to suggest ways in which society may use the work of psychologists, and to explore the prospects for psychologists to increase their usefulness. Our recommendations are addressed primarily to persons who can influence the future of psychology most: those who support our research, those who can influence the education of psychologists and their employment, those who are potential users of psychological information and methods, and those who by entering the field might strengthen it.

This report is the work of a panel that was convened as part of a larger examination of all of the behavioral and social sciences. Our task was simplified by the work of the Central Planning Committee of the Behavioral and Social Sciences Survey Committee, and by the active participation in our deliberations of the three leading members of that group: Drs. E. R. Hilgard, Henry W. Riecken, and Stephen Viederman. We are in their debt for both their guidance and their work on our panel's assignment.

Our procedures have been similar to those of our sister panels in the behavioral and social sciences. We have queried our colleagues in the universities about their plans and their problems. We have discussed the needs of the field among ourselves and with many concerned persons. Here we report our conclusions, emphasizing some by making explicit recommendations. We have tried to support our

1

recommendations and to make them meaningful by providing examples of the work of psychologists and by describing how psychologists are educated and employed.

The report begins with a statement about the nature of the work of psychologists, their numbers, and their distribution in the general population. The next eight chapters describe the work of psychologists, and the samplings included are designed to indicate the diversity of the fields. Three chapters follow relating information about the numbers of qualified psychologists, about the ways in which they are supported in their research activities, and about the problems they face in universities in their programs of teaching and research. We conclude with a number of recommendations aimed at increasing the quality of psychology as a science and its value as a profession in service to individuals and society.

The Appendix contains a list of the educational psychology and psychology departments that participated in the questionnaire survey described in the Foreword. Those who want to read more extensively about psychology may wish to consult the Suggested Readings section. The reader might also refer to current introductory textbooks.

Many persons and institutions have helped in the preparation of this report. Financial support came from the Russell Sage Foundation, the National Science Foundation, the National Institute of Health, and the National Institute of Mental Health. We are indebted to several persons not on our panel who helped to write the various sections of the report:

> Dr. William Kessen, *Yale University*
> Dr. Floyd R. Ratcliff, *Rockefeller University*
> Dr. Stuart W. Cook, *University of Colorado*
> Dr. Leonard Krasner, *State University of New York at Stony Brook*

A large number of persons read portions of this report or aided in the improvement of the information presented. Among these readers we are especially indebted to

> Dr. Harvey Brooks, *Harvard University*
> Dr. Peter Elias, *Massachusetts Institute of Technology*

Dr. Howard Hines, *National Science Foundation*
Dr. Howard H. Kendler, *University of California at Santa Barbara*
Dr. Rensis Likert, *University of Michigan*
Dr. William J. McGuire, *University of California at San Diego*
Dr. A. Kimball Romney, *University of California at Irvine*
Dr. Eli A. Rubinstein, *National Institute of Mental Health*
Dr. Harold Sigall, *University of Rochester*
Dr. Herbert A. Simon, *Carnegie-Mellon University*

We are greatly indebted to Mrs. Miriam Rock of the University of Rochester for assistance in the editorial review of the contents of this report.

1
INTRODUCTION

The nature of psychology today belies its origins as an offshoot of philosophy. Even its name, which means the study of the soul or mind, is no longer adequate. Currently psychology is concerned with organisms from the flatworm to man, with phenomena ranging from prenatal conditioning to brain changes in senility, and with processes as simple as the eye blink or as complex as man's adaptation to an environment in outer space.

Psychology is usually defined as the scientific study of behavior. Its subject matter includes behavioral processes that are observable, such as gestures, speech, and physiological changes, and processes that can only be inferred, such as thoughts and dreams. Psychology occupies a crucial position among the disciplines that endeavor to understand man scientifically. It is in part a life science, closely related to biology and psychiatry, for it studies the behavior and mental functions of living organisms. It is also a social science, related to anthropology, sociology, and political science, for it deals with behavior in complex social environments. It is also a profession dedicated to the application of psychological knowledge and techniques to human problems.

Psychologists employ no single technique to study behavior, but they rely generally on the analytical and conceptual methods shared by all scientists. They may make their approach from the biological point of view and investigate the evolutionary and neurological basis of animal and human behavior (see Chapters 2 and 3 and the more

5

extensive report of the Behavioral Biology Panel of the Committee on Research in the Life Sciences*). They may observe and record incidents of behavior, as developmental psychologists working with children have done for many years. They may count particular responses in varying circumstances, as students of verbal behavior have done to show the influence of another's approval on speech patterns. They may ask questions and summarize answers into test scores, as hundreds of administrators of intelligence tests have done for the last sixty years. They may observe the changes in behavior produced by rewards, as many investigators of conditioning and learning have done. Using statistical analyses they may compare the characteristic responses of one group with those of another. They may spend many hours trying to understand the reasons for a particular pattern of behavior in one person, as many clinical psychologists do in work with their clients. They may examine an operating social system to discover how its effectiveness might be improved, as many management psychologists do.

In the United States today, there are about 75,000 persons whose day-to-day work involves a substantial portion of activities that one would call psychological; there are 40,000 psychological practitioners (not all with PhDs) and 9,000 clinical psychologists with PhD degrees working with individuals or with groups, or in some unit of business, education, or government. They are engaged increasingly in aiding workers and their employers, consumers and producers of goods, teachers and students, engineers and machine operators, managers of psychiatric care and their patients. They have served in government, in industry, in schools, colleges, and universities, in hospitals and clinics, and in private practice where they have helped many individuals deal with their personal problems in face-to-face relations.

Psychology contributes to mental health. Many psychologists work in close association with psychiatrists on the problems of diagnosis, care, and treatment of persons with neurotic and psychotic symptoms. Their competence in research techniques and in evaluative procedures adds a valuable dimension to the medical skills of the psychiatrist in studies of mental illness and health. Psychological

* The Committee on Research in the Life Sciences is a parallel of the Behavioral and Social Sciences Survey Committee. Its panel reports will be published in one volume by Oxford University Press in 1970.

tests have been developed not only to identify persons with disorders but also to sort out those more likely to benefit from treatment and to assess its effects. Psychologists work with psychiatrists on the development and evaluation of new modes of treatment for persons in hospitals and clinics and with psychiatrists and pharmacologists to discover ways in which new drugs can be used to benefit the mentally ill. Today a large part of individual psychotherapy is provided by psychologists, with an expanding amount of this work related to increasing the happiness of individuals rather than solely to reduce psychological disability.

Psychology contributes to education. Approximately 12,000 psychologists are employed in teaching and research in colleges and universities. Of these only about 2,500 are employed in the 120 departments of psychology that awarded the PhD degree during the ten years preceding this report. About one psychologist in ten is employed in a school system. Large numbers of psychologists have been attracted to work in school systems in the improvement of teaching methods, in the development of new teaching devices, and in the study of social and emotional problems. A school psychologist may work as a clinician with individual problem cases in the school or with particular instances of learning disorders. He may work as a researcher collecting data on the effectiveness of various educational programs. He may be primarily responsible for the administration and interpretation of tests or for the evaluation of the overall educational program of the school.

Psychology contributes to business and industry. Psychologists working as advisors and consultants, as well as direct employees, have strongly influenced the methods of personnel selection in many industries. They have analyzed and modified management procedures and have assisted both labor and management in avoiding or resolving conflicts of interests. Their research has strongly influenced merchandising and advertising programs.

Psychology contributes to government. Many psychologists are employed by federal and state governments, usually in the Civil Service Commission or in employment services, but also in research or planning in agencies engaged in programs of social development. The Department of Defense, for example, employs a large number of psychologists in the evaluation of training programs, in the identification and utilization of individual talents of persons in military service, in the development of systems for training persons to perform specific tasks, in testing the appropriateness of food and clothing for soldiers, in the design and improvement of equipment to match the abilities of a user, and in studies aimed at aiding both the making of policy and its implementation in military programs.

Psychology contributes to communities. In recent years psychologists increasingly have been drawn into community activities to aid in providing ample educational and occupational opportunities to all citizens. Their studies have demonstrated the importance of early language training in the home, the devastating effects of teachers' negative attitudes on students' learning, the need to humanize education, and the effects of extreme cultural deprivation on the development of abilities.

Psychologists who serve in these varied roles use the findings of psychological science to assist them in their work. They also generate new findings, since many social problems cannot be characterized or resolved by the direct application of existing psychological knowledge. Often a psychologist settles on a new method of attack and, by careful assessment of his results, adds an increment to knowledge. In this role he does what a creative engineer often does in the design of a new machine. Unlike the engineer, the psychologist often discovers that too little basic science exists to assure him that a given approach will work. Since a human being in his social context is far more complex than the most intricate mechanisms yet devised by man, the psychologist frequently solves his problem less effectively than does the engineer.

Today there is a great interest in efforts to make psychological science more useful to the society supporting it. One way often proposed is to persuade psychologists to devote themselves single-mindedly to solving those problems the public deems most urgent, dedicating their scientific talents solely to problems of peace, poverty, education, mental health, population control, or other important social issues. But attention directed solely at solving immediate practical problems would lead to unfortunate consequences for the science, and, in the long run, would lessen its usefulness. Few social problems are easily transformed into scientific problems. Before a scientist is ready to contribute to a socially defined problem, he must find a way to analyze and translate the problem so the methods and concepts of science will be applicable. Analysis and translation are arts in themselves.

Another approach may be equally effective. Many psychologists maintain that successful laboratory attacks on behavioral problems occur most readily when they are pursued without regard to their immediate usefulness. They point out that to deal with a problem directly in terms of its social importance may be frustrating because it is usually so difficult to formulate the problem in scientifically tractable terms.

The history of psychology provides ample support for proceeding along both lines. Some of the psychological research discussed in the following chapters was initiated in the laboratory; other studies began as attempts to solve practical problems. There is little indication that research inspired by social needs has been more successful in solving problems of society than has research that followed simply as the next logical step in a program of investigation. Urging all psychologists to devote their full energies to solving current social crises would be a poor way to insure that their work would be of maximum social benefit. Not only is a balance between basic and applied approaches required, but insistence on social relevance by those who provide financial support for psychology must be tempered with good judgment. It is almost a truism that the psychologist, not the would-be beneficiary of his findings, is best equipped to formulate fruitful questions for psychological research. Yet among psychologists engaged in asking interesting scientific questions, many will choose to work on questions directly responsive to social needs.

Evidence is accumulating to suggest that it is possible to analyze practical problems faced by social managers in local, state, and federal government, in business and industry, in educational, medical, military, and other contexts and to translate them so that psychological knowledge can be applied. This has occurred when the psychologist was an active participant in a team of workers dealing with problems in a social setting. Today the most effective coupling of psychological science and social needs is probably accomplished by individuals trained in psychology who have specialized in scientific administration and management. We need many more people with this dual training.

Much psychological knowledge can be used to improve the effectiveness of our social programs. Leaders who accept the responsibility for implementing those programs require an advanced understanding of the applicable principles of psychology. If they hold the traditional beliefs of our culture about the nature of man, their programs may perpetuate the problems they are trying to alleviate. There is a great need to train people who participate in these programs to use the findings of psychology, to recognize, for example, that there are vast differences among individuals, that a person's conduct is strongly influenced by social pressures, that rewards are more effective than punishments in encouraging socially acceptable behavior, that time and resources for solving our problems are strictly limited, that conflict can be avoided or resolved by methods of persuasion and negotiation, that the way people see a situation is more important to them than are the facts, and that human motivation is so complex that one seldom does anything for a single reason.

More than lip-service acceptance of these views is required; they must be built into programs, procedures, and routines of action. Means and methods of interaction between social managers and psychological scientists can be institutionalized more efficiently than are our current practices. We should begin to search for such an institutional solution, by initiating for example, a study of how and where such a match is succeeding most imaginatively and competently, with the expectation that the most effective methods might be adopted elsewhere. Even a cursory consideration of the problem indicates that new career patterns are needed to provide scientific training and experience in applying psychology along with managerial skills; individuals with such experience exist, but the relatively low prestige accorded them by the community of academic psychologists suggests that their contribution is not properly appreciated and that their number is unlikely to grow commensurate with our need for their services.

The challenging problem of serving the needs of society better cannot be restricted solely to the field of psychology. A scientific program that will deal capably with a social need will not remain neatly tucked inside the disciplinary boundaries set by professional societies and university departments. Whole teams of behavioral and social scientists, engineers, biologists, physicists, and other scientific and technical personnel—not just psychologists alone—will be required to tackle social problems effectively.

Important things are happening in psychology. Increasingly students are attracted to the field. They are excited by the challenge of dealing directly with individual and social problems and the potential of psychology to meet that challenge. The lure of psychology is a cause for great concern to universities today. Growing numbers of applicants are asking for admission to graduate schools, but graduate departments of psychology are growing too slowly to absorb them. The better graduate departments are receiving over thirty applications for every vacancy. Since the cost of providing education for each student is substantial, the likelihood of reducing this ratio very much in the near future is not great. On the contrary, the problem can be expected to grow more serious as the character of psychology changes and its influence extends. The impact of the socially heightened consciousness of the younger members of our society can already be seen in the changing patterns of research in all of psychology. Not only is there a desire to gain a better understanding of the strong social forces that produce turmoil, but new findings and new techniques suggest that we will be better able to deal with these forces and to gain some control over them.

A substantial number of major programs for social improvement in this country rely upon a set of assumptions about human characteristics which are based on knowledge of varying degrees of accuracy about the nature of man. Any examination and resultant revision in our established pattern of education and our system of law and justice requires scientific rather than hearsay evidence as a basis for judgment.

2
THE BIOLOGICAL BASIS
OF BEHAVIOR

OUR BIOLOGICAL HERITAGE

A large portion of psychology is essentially a part of biology, but with behavior the important object of study. A comparative study of the behavior of different organisms aids in understanding the effects of one's biological heritage on his capabilities to learn or to adjust to environmental change.

The procedures for the study of behavior involve field observation of different species of organisms in their natural habitat, observation of them in controlled environments, or direct study where conditions can be experimentally controlled or varied. A biological approach provides a somewhat different perspective by comparing man with the so-called lower animals and so provides a better understanding of man and his behavior.

The study of the psychology of animals has several advantages. One is that animals often provide simpler cases for study than can be found in human behavior. For example, maternal or sexual behavior in birds and mammals provides simple instances of these behaviors without the complications by human culture. Sometimes animal behavior shows a striking similarity to human behavior. When mother love and peer group association are withdrawn from an infant monkey, it develops behavior defects which resemble those seen in the human; the infant monkey, like a neglected child, fails to grow and thrive normally. Later in life its social reactions to other

12

monkeys are abnormal and parenthood is unlikely and at best pathological. In other species such as dogs, however, an infant separated early from its mother grows and thrives normally. This is also the case for sheep; a lamb shows no tendency to return to its natural mother (or to other sheep) after it has been separated from them for as little as twelve hours. There are some extreme cases of biological and behavioral specialization. The death of the male spider after mating or the death of the female salmon after laying her eggs are two such examples. Yet such cases of specialization are often instructive just because they are different from what is observed in man.

Not only do animals provide simpler cases of behavior, but careful extrapolation from studies of animal behavior can often prove of great value in the study of man. For instance, laboratory studies with animals have shown that severe malnutrition early in life not only stunts growth but also impairs development of the central nervous system. In a world where two-thirds of the children suffer from protein deficiency, the potential significance of such studies for man cannot be overlooked. To take another example, there has always been a serious concern as to the extent that castration or ovariectomy influences sexual behavior in man. After the loss of the sex hormones, some patients lose all sexual interest but others do not. Comparative studies of rats, cats, dogs, and monkeys show a decreasing dependence on sex hormones in this series and an increasing dependence on sensory stimulation and cortical brain function. Man seems even less dependent on sex hormones for sexual arousal. More and more evidence indicates that the lack of sexual interest after castration may be a secondary effect of fear and negative suggestion. Indeed, there is sometimes a loss of sexuality after vasectomy, performed for sterilization purposes, even though this procedure does not affect hormonal levels.

A third reason for studying the behavior of animals is their accessibility for procedures and experiments not readily applicable to man. For example, in studying the effects of brain injury or brain tumors, it is a great advantage to be able to make experimental lesions or tumors in the brains of animals to learn what behavioral effects are produced and how the defects may be overcome. In fact, some of our best ideas for procedures to treat the accidentally brain-injured human have come from investigations of experimentally produced brain lesions in animals.

Finally, it should be pointed out that we also study animal behavior because we are interested in animal behavior itself. Animals comprise a large part of our natural environment and have always been an object of man's curiosity. By studying animal behavior we are better able to use animals for our economic purposes. For example, the discovery that most of the weight loss of cattle during shipment is due to emotionality which can be overcome by the use of tranquilizers during shipment has been of considerable economic value.

The biological mechanisms underlying behavior not only affect our analysis of behavioral organization, they provide tools for further modification and evaluation of behavior. A few examples will illustrate the importance of this approach and its implication.

Heredity and Genetic Mechanisms

Genetic mechanisms play an important role in determining the behavior of animals and men. Some behavior occurs without the benefit of specific, relevant prior experience. This is the so-called innate or species-specific behavior. Such simple behavior patterns as walking, swimming, and flying can be shown to develop without prior training. For example, if salamanders are anesthetized just before they have begun to swim and are held under anesthesia past the time when they would normally be swimming, when released from anesthesia they swim in a normal pattern, showing that this behavior can emerge without the benefit of experience. A more complex example of species-specific behavior is the fear reaction shown by young ducks or geese when a silhouette in the pattern of a hawk is sailed over their heads. If the same silhouette sails in the opposite direction, it resembles a goose, which elicits no fear reaction. However, a specific bit of behavior reflects the influence of prior experience. At first the young bird responds to any moving large silhouette but habituates to those that occur frequently. Thus birds raised in a free environment habituate to other types of birds flying overhead but not to the hawk which occurs relatively rarely.

Bird songs provide further examples. Certain birds raised in isolation sing the song of their species in every detail. Other species, however, require a certain amount of experience before being able to sing their own song. If these birds are raised in isolation, they will either not sing or will sing only a portion of the song typical of their species. In fact, some birds will adopt the song of other species with which they are raised. Although the influence of an hereditary mechanism may be recognized, it interacts with other influences to determine behavior.

Another approach to genetic mechanisms is to breed animals selectively for high or low levels of such types of behavior as activity, emotionality, or learning ability. Strains of rats can be selectively bred so that one strain learns mazes slowly and the other learns them rapidly. The slow learners have smaller brains and somewhat different brain chemistry than the rapid learners.

It has long been suspected that similar genetic mechanisms influence human behavior. A predisposition to schizophrenia is dependent upon heredity mechanisms. Brothers and sisters of schizophrenics have a greater chance of developing the disease than would be predicted from its incidence in the general population. The occurrence in fraternal twins, who are no more similar genetically than ordinary brothers and sisters, is no greater than among brothers and sisters. Studies of identical twins, with an identical genetic makeup, show that if one twin has schizophrenia the chances are high that the other twin will also, even if they have been reared apart from infancy. More direct is the case of phenylketonuria, for in this type of mental retardation it has been shown that a single recessive gene is responsible. The gene involved directs the metabolism of phenylalanine, an amino acid important in brain metabolism.

In all of these cases we see the contribution of the genetic mechanism; environment and experience may also play important roles in behavior depending upon the amount and rigorousness of genetic preprogramming.

Species-Specific Behavior

Both in field observations and laboratory studies, many different kinds of behavior may be seen which in their specific form are typical of a given species. These may account for the control of population levels, the establishment of territory, the segregation of species by preventing crossbreeding; they can also account for mating, care of the young, feeding, diet selection, temperature regulations (such as hibernation or burrowing), communication, and in some instances homing and migration.

The interaction between parents and their offspring is a complex behavioral process dependent upon innate mechanisms in the mother and father as well as in the offspring. Learning and experience can be important, but so can the internal state of the animal. For example, young ducks follow their own parents selectively. When a colony is aroused by a predator and the adults scurry in every direction for cover, the young sort themselves out and follow their own parents. The ability to recognize the parent depends on experience of the young duckling in the first few hours of life after hatching. In fact it turns out to be not at all a genetic matter, specific to parents, but rather a matter of what moving stimulus the young duckling sees first upon emerging from the egg. If the young duck first sees a person or a moving box on a trolley wire it will become imprinted on these unnatural objects and will follow them in preference to its own biological parents. If imprinting does not occur within the first two days of life, if hatching occurs in isolation, then it will not occur at all.

Animals develop territories which they defend by keeping out competitors and other intruders. Sometimes this occurs in connection with mating, sometimes in connection with the care of the young, and sometimes in connection with defense of the social group. In all instances communication, vocal or gestural, is involved. For example, a male stickleback (a fish) will defend its territory by attacking any male competitor. The crucial environmental stimulus which elicits the attack behavior is not the shape of the male competitor but rather the red color of its underbelly. The attack behavior can be elicited by a model that does not have the shape of a stickleback but has the red belly. In this species, aggression is controlled by a very specific stimulus pattern. Similar specificity has been observed in many other animal species. Moreover, there are behavior patterns that can call off an attack as well as provoke one. If in a hostile encounter of two wolves one lies on his back and exposes his throat in a helpless position, the attacking wolf will stop his attack.

Species-specific behavior patterns contribute in a major way to the social organization of animal groups. Some of the most important and common stimulus patterns for eliciting species-specific behavior are provided by the behavior of another animal, by a mate, an offspring, a dominant male, or even a predator. Many species-specific behavior patterns guide and direct the social relation among individuals in specific ways. The song of a bird not only attracts a mate but drives off competitors of the same sex. In a single set of gestures and vocalizations, a dominant male monkey can cause his females and young to retreat into a protective cluster and at the same time hold a strange intruder at bay. This kind of communication by gesture and other eliciting behavior often precludes physical contact and injury in the natural social setting, as witness the success of the posture of "helplessness" in the wolf or the flight-from-a-distance response of the submissive animal to the sight and posture of the dominant animal.

The Social Psychology of Animals

The interdependence of various parts of psychology is perhaps no where better illustrated than in the conjunctions between social psychology and the study of non-human behavior, especially that of animals and insects. Although the domiciliary habits of insects, particularly ants and bees, occupied the attention of some social scientists in the late nineteenth century, during the early part of the twentieth century the study of animal social behavior fell largely outside the interests of social scientists, including social psychologists. There were experimental studies of imitation and cooperation by rats and laboratory research on both aggressive and competitive behavior, but somehow the essentially social aspects of this behavior were neglected. Following World War II, the work of the European ethologists, especially Niko Tinbergen and Konrad Lorenz, led to renewed study of animal social behavior. Almost simultaneously there grew up the work of primatologists, many of whom were anthropologists. Both approaches emphasize the study of animals in natural settings and communities, and they have made clear the enormous importance of social life for subhuman animals. Our previous assessment of baboon behavior had been distorted by the baboons' captivity. Whereas baboons in zoos seemed to be primarily concerned with sexual behavior, animals in their natural habitat were clearly more concerned with the social organization of the troop and with getting food. Studies of elk in North America and of the large ungulates of central India further confirmed the importance of natural communities and their socializing effects.

Social psychological methods and concepts have not yet been integrated into research on animal behavior to any great extent. Nevertheless it is obvious that animal social behavior holds enormous interest for social psychologists. Although the temptation to generalize directly from animal to human societies is very strong, it should be resisted. For example, studies of overcrowding in animal communities, which show reduced sexual activity, lower birth rates, and a higher incidence of degenerative diseases, do not parallel the human experience of urban crowding. In comparison with the population as a whole, the ghetto dweller shows a higher rate of sexual activity, a higher birth rate, and a lower incidence of degenerative diseases. He is, on the other hand, more afflicted by communicable diseases such as tuberculosis. Lower birth rate and higher degenerative disease rate would probably be found among the upper classes living in less crowded conditions. Could it be that the experience of stress is greater for upper class humans than for lower class, and greater for crowded animals than for uncrowded? Whatever the answer to this particular question, it is evident that animal behavior research is moving into the range of human social psychology, and one can look forward to collaboration between these two seemingly distant branches of the psychological enterprise.

To summarize, the deepest roots of human behavior lie in man's inherited biological machinery. By studying animals in the field and in the laboratory psychologists and other students of behavior can increase their understanding of the biological bases of aggression, territoriality, mating, care of the young, and other social behaviors. The study of animals permits not only the examination of simple models of behavior, but also allows direct investigation of the biological machinery itself. Experiments on animals can control the life history of the organism or intervene surgically or chemically in the organism's underlying physiology. From such investigations, principles of behavior can emerge that should give us new perspectives on our human condition and our human society.

BRAIN AND BEHAVIOR

The study of the behavior of organisms has led inevitably to an examination of the brain and its relation to consciousness, memory, sleep, fatigue, hearing and seeing, hunger and thirst, and emotions. The mysteries of mind and body relationships long eluded objective investigation. Today, the nature of those relationships is being studied by means of an entirely new set of procedures and techniques considered impossible as little as fifty years ago.

Early studies of the brain, undertaken primarily by neurologists and anatomists, were essentially taxonomic. The gross structure of the brain was well known for centuries; the detailed cellular structure has become quite well known during this century. Study of the structure alone, however, has been limited in value, not only because of the huge number of cells to be identified (there are 14 billion neurons in the brain) but also because microscopic study alone indicates function only indirectly.

The nature of the human brain has also been studied by neurosurgeons as they have exposed and operated upon the brain to remove tumors or to correct other disorders. Recording of brain activity, or of stimulating various parts of the exposed human brain provided direct and useful information on the distribution of various functions in different areas of the brain.

Fascination with many unanswered questions about brain and behavior has impelled many psychologists to master surgical techniques and to team up with physiologists, neurologists, biochemists, and anatomists to examine, usually in lower animals, the workings of the brain. In some studies, using rats, cats, or monkeys, portions of the brain were removed, or electrodes were carefully implanted, or small amounts of chemicals were introduced into a special area of the brain.

Studies of this sort require investigators with highly developed surgical skills, histologists to check on the correctness of electrode locations, psychologists able to assess behavioral effects, and laboratories equipped with computers, operating rooms, electronic equipment for behavioral control and recording, animal laboratories and colony rooms, and, in some instances, biochemical laboratories. Psychologists working in these settings require much more training and more support than did the early philosophers who conjectured about the probable seat of consciousness, or mind, in the human organism. The findings of today's students may not sound like the answers given by early philosophers to this question, but they are equally interesting.

The brain is the locus of emotions, such as love, fear, and rage, and of drives, such as thirst and hunger, which are now known to originate from it rather than from peripheral sensations such as the dryness of the mouth or the contractions of the stomach. The brain analyzes information from our sense organs to provide an orderly basis for our perception of the world about us. It achieves the coordination of our motor movements. It retrieves appropriate memories, plans for the future, thinks, and reasons creatively. The brain is the supreme organ of integration, and there are many beautiful relations among these apparently diverse functions.

The activity of the nervous system is self-regulating in that it can control its own internal chemical and physical environment; it selectively monitors the information it receives, it modulates its own motor output, and it receives constant feedback from the consequences of its own activity. It is likely that the complex processes of attention, consciousness, and subjective cognitive and affective experience are products of this self-regulating activity of the nervous system.

The brain was once thought of as a great but passive switchboard activated only when stimulated by peripheral sense organs. (Given the stimulus, what is the response?) But the brain plays far more of a role in behavior than that. Now we know that each signal generated in a sense organ and entering the brain impinges on a background of spontaneous activity, is modified by and in turn modifies this ongoing activity. In addition to pathways from the sense organs to the brain, there are pathways from the brain to various sensory relay stations and even to the sense organs themselves. Impulses going out over these pathways can weaken, or even completely inhibit, messages coming in from the sense organs. This gives the brain a way to control its own input. The discovery of this function of the brain has helped us to understand the mechanism of selective attention, which permits a person to "tune out" many incoming signals that otherwise would make the world little more than a buzzing confusion.

In addition to its connections with the sense organs that respond to the external world, certain cells in the brain function as sense organs to monitor the internal states of our body. By detecting variables such as temperature and the concentration of salt in the blood, they help the brain to regulate the vital functions essential to our health. Part of this regulation takes place by the nerves from the brain to the body. But the brain also functions similarly to a gland by secreting chemical messengers that are sent to other parts of the body. It responds to hormones from the body and helps to regulate the secretion of such hormones. It is no accident that the master gland, the pituitary, is located at the base of the brain from which it receives both neural and chemical regulation.

Physiological psychology is the study of how simple and complex behavioral processes are produced by the nervous system in its interactions with the rest of the body. Although the advances in our knowledge of physiological psychology have been enormous in the last fifty years, the field is still in its infancy. In order to suggest how far we have come and how far we have yet to go, we can outline some major achievements physiological psychology has made in both technique and concept and then point to the major scientific problems that physiological psychology now faces. For this purpose, it will be simplest to use the classical organization of psychology into sensation and perception; motor organization and response mechanisms; motivation and emotion; learning and memory; and the complex processes of intelligence, symbolic process, reasoning, thinking, attention, and consciousness.

Sensation and Perception

The traditional approach to understanding sensation and perception has been to specify the anatomical and physiological properties of receptor organs and to trace the sensory pathways going from them into the central nervous system. The classic doctrine of "specific nerve energies" expressed the notion that different qualities of sensation arise from the activity of different receptors (or different parts of the same receptor) and remain segregated in different parts of the central nervous system. Anatomical findings have supported these traditional notions only to a degree. Electrophysiological recordings from peripheral nerves have shown that the same anatomical pathways may contain nerves of different conduction velocities and different response characteristics that could also code sensory qualities.

Modern attempts to relate the qualities of sensation to both anatomical and physiological properties of receptors and their sensory nerves are well illustrated by the case of hearing. Teams of investigators have used precise equipment to observe specific events in each part of the auditory system from the outer ear to the auditory cortex. They have devised systems of stimulation and observation to identify the role of each part of the system and have studied detailed sections of each part of the system. This massive effort indicated clearly the way in which complex sounds are transmitted so as to be meaningful when perceived by the individual.

Sound waves are transmitted through movements of the eardrum and the auditory ossicles to standing waves in the fluid of the cochlea of the ear. These standing waves move different parts of the auditory receptive surface on the basilar membrane of the cochlea, depending upon the frequency of the waves. Such selective movement of the basilar membrane causes distortions of its receptor cells in relatively specific locations, and distortions of the receptor cells generate minute electric currents which probably stimulate neighboring auditory nerve fibers according to the frequency of the waves. The degree of selectivity would be relatively crude except for the fact that each frequency of stimulation generates both excitatory and inhibitory nerve activity, with the result that selective excitation of auditory nerve fibers is sharpened.

Recording from sensory areas within the central nervous system has revealed more complex mechanisms for selective response to patterns of sensory input. For example, in the visual system individual neurons have been found that are selectively responsive to edges, to borders, to the orientation of lines, and to the direction of movement. In experiments involving stimulation of the two eyes, neurons have been found that respond to convergent information, possibly revealing the central nervous mechanisms underlying such complex perceptual processes as depth perception and interocular reactions.

Even more complex sensory mechanisms are revealed by experiments on individuals who have suffered specific (selective) brain damage. For example, destruction of the visual cortex virtually eliminates any capacity to appreciate visual detail and pattern and greatly alters the appreciation of differences in brightness. Other central nervous system damage outside the primary sensory areas—in the neighboring association cortex, for example—can result in even more complex perceptual defects. Tumors may result in a condition known as agnosia; a patient may be able to describe the shape and color of an orange, but not able to say what it is, for example.

Many problems remain to be solved concerning the basis of sensation and perception: How is energy transduced in a sense organ and how does the sense organ give rise to nerve impulses? How do anatomical locus and physiological patterns of nerve discharge contribute to qualities of sensation and perception? How are sensory experience and behavioral discrimination produced by the interaction of central neural structures at various levels of the sensory system?

Knowledge of the relationship between the events of the external world and the way they are perceived by an individual requires more than an understanding of the way in which information is transmitted from sense organ to the brain. Obviously, it requires knowledge about past experience and current brain states. The work done thus far has aided our understanding of the effects of drugs on sensory experience and has suggested ways to improve sensory defects, such as hearing loss. It has also suggested methods for improving the presentation of signals to an individual to increase the likelihood of evoking the desired response. It is evident that further work in this area may provide artificial sensing devices for the blind or deaf far superior to those now extant; and it will greatly improve our understanding of how man makes order out of the mass of chaotic sensory input that he must process.

Motivation and Emotion

The nervous system undergoes complex changes in its level of activity and arousal. These changes are strikingly illustrated in the physiological and behavioral manifestations of sleep, but the nervous system may also be aroused in highly specific ways in hunger, rage, or sexual behavior, for example. These specific arousals underlie the behavioral qualities that psychologists tend to call drive and biologists call instinct. Under such conditions, an organism's central neural mechanisms are highly selective, as illustrated by the hungry animal's selective response to food, and its specific response mechanisms are "primed" and highly "energized," as illustrated by the low threshold for arousal of sexual reflexes in a receptive female cat.

The central neural mechanisms of many drives and certain kinds of emotions are now reasonably well understood. There appears to be a focus of such mechanisms in the hypothalamus, deep in the brain. Experimental analysis shows that these hypothalamic mechanisms are not only responsive to sensory stimuli but also to changes in the internal environment, that is the blood and other body fluids. For example, sex hormones which are so important in the arousal of mating behavior in the lower mammals affect the anterior hypothalamus and preoptic area. In one experiment, done on the castrated rat, a minute quantity of sex hormone was implanted in the brain tissue. The result was that a sexually unresponsive male rat was aroused to immediate and vigorous sexual activity in the presence of a receptive female. It is significant that the region of the hypothalamus concerned with the hormonal elicitation of sexual behavior is anatomically separated from the region concerned with the physiological control of the sex glands.

There is another, nearby, region of the brain—the lateral hypothalamus—where a few millionths of an ampere of electrical stimulation can elicit eating. In order to study this area, electrodes are implanted under surgical anesthesia and cemented to the skull, so that after the animal has completely recovered, he can be stimulated in his normal, waking state. When the lateral hypothalamus is gently stimulated, a rat that has been completely satiated on food will eat. But when his brain is stimulated more strongly, he may gnaw a stick. How can we tell whether the electrical stimulation is eliciting only reflex gnawing which looks like hunger when food is present or is eliciting true hunger, perhaps making the rat so hungry that he will even try to eat the stick? One way is to make the rat normally hungry by taking away all of his food for a while and then training him to learn to find food by pressing back a little panel which hides it. After he has learned this, we satiate him by letting him eat all the food he wants. Then we test the effect of stimulating his brain. If the stimulation is merely eliciting reflex gnawing, it will cause him to bite something; if it is eliciting true hunger, it will cause him to perform his newly learned habit.

The rat sits quietly until the current is turned on and then performs the newly learned habit of pushing back the panel to get the food. When the current is turned off, he stops. A number of tests such as this have proven conclusively that stimulation of this small area of the brain has all the properties of the normal hunger drive. Furthermore, destroying this tiny area of the brain has the opposite effect to that of stimulation; it causes the rat to stop eating and starve. Therefore, we call this the feeding area of the lateral hypothalamus, and conclude that it is an important part of the hierarchy of food regulating systems in the brain. But this area of the hypothalamus overlaps considerably with a thirst area where stimulation will elicit drinking of water and destruction will cause the animal to stop drinking till it dies.

Stimulation in another nearby area of the hypothalamus, namely, the ventromedial nucleus, causes hungry rats to stop eating. Destroying this area has the opposite effect of causing rats to overeat until they become grossly fat. Thus, hunger is regulated by two areas of the brain, the first of which is excitatory and the second of which is inhibitory. This example illustrates how we are learning something about the brain mechanisms controlling motivation. It also illustrates how the brain uses complementary controls, one excitatory and one inhibitory, which are balanced against each other.

Learning and Memory

It is axiomatic in physiological psychology that learning represents a change in the structure and function of the nervous system and that memory signifies that the change is an enduring one. Efforts to localize the changes that take place in learning—by destroying parts of the brain or by recording electrical activity of the brain during learning—have shown that many different parts of the brain are involved. However, there are now a group of observations and experiments that focus special attention upon the temporal lobes and the hippocampal and amygdaloid structures contained within them. For example, epileptic discharge within the temporal lobe of the human patient often results in amnesia or other memory impairment. In patients that have temporal lobe epilepsy it has been found that electrical stimulation in the vicinity of critical area is capable of eliciting memories. Furthermore, neurosurgical procedures which result in bilateral damage to the temporal lobe will produce memory defects. The presumption is that the temporal lobe has particular control over diffusely located learning and memory mechanisms in the brain.

Scientists have advanced various theories concerning the nature of the physical change that occurs in the brain in the course of learning. Most attention has been directed at the synapse, the area where the ends of two or more neurons come close enough together to permit the transmission of impulses. Most of these theories are little more than conjecture, usually postulating a change in structure or in chemical state. The recent remarkable success of research showing that genetic information can be encoded in the large protein molecule DNA has led many theorists to favor the notion that RNA may be the macromolecule involved in recording the effects of learning.

One effect of this suggestion his been the profitable addition of biochemists to the usual teams of investigators studying the physiological basis for learning. As a result of joining psychologists, biochemists, and histologists into a team, we may see some carefully controlled studies that will provide spectacular advances in our understanding of how learning occurs and how it may be facilitated. This problem area is surely one of the most promising of all areas of science today.

Some experiments have already been successful. For example, it has been shown in a number of laboratories that the antibiotic puromycin will eliminate memory in both the mouse and the goldfish if injected directly into the brain following a learning experience.

This puromycin effect appears to be specific to recent memory and does not seem to have any effect upon long standing memory or the capacity of the animal to make organized responses.

The puromycin experiments suggest that memory requires considerable time to form within the brain, because during a period of approximately two days memory is vulnerable to injection of puromycin into the temporal lobe and after six days it is not. Putting this result together with findings of experiments in which animals are given electroconvulsive shock at various times after learning leads to the hypothesis that memory may be a multistage phenomenon. Establishing a memory may involve initial stages requiring only milli-seconds, other stages requiring seconds or minutes, and still other stages requiring hours or days for their completion. If this hypothesis is correct, it would also be reasonable to believe that different stages of memory formation, marked by such widely different times, may actually represent different biological processes. The short-term processes may well be a temporary physiological effect; the longer processes may be chemical; and the permanent processes may indeed represent anatomical changes. Although much of this thinking is still speculative, there is reason to believe that these different mechanisms may be at work in different loci of the brain at different times.

Complex Processes

The neurological basis of complex mental processes poses a most difficult problem because it is not easy to use animal subjects in the investigation of such behavioral processes as attention, symbolic processes, reasoning, and consciousness. In addition to the headway made in animal work, there are instructive human cases to be found in the neurological clinic. For example, it has been found that there are mechanisms in the brain stem which may play an important role in attention and consciousness. These mechanisms are located in the reticular formation of the brain stem. They serve both in the arousal of the electrical activity of the brain and in general behavioral arousal. The reticular formation is a complex mass of nerve fibers, receiving collaterals from all the main sensory pathways. It is generally believed that when an animal receives sensory stimulation, the main, long sensory pathways carry specific, coded information to the forebrain, and that at the same time the collaterals leading to the reticular formation serve the function of arousing structures in the forebrain that must handle the incoming specific sensory information. Damage to the reticular formation results in an animal that is initially unconscious or asleep and later drowsy and inattentive as it recovers from the acute effects of the operation. Conversely, stimulation of the reticular formation while a monkey is doing a perceptual task has shown that performance can be enhanced.

In human patients remarkable cases have been described in which frontal lobe lesions have caused an inability to understand abstract ideas that are easily executed in concrete form. For example, a patient with damage to his frontal lobes can easily drink a glass of water, but he cannot make believe that he is drinking from an empty glass. In other cases, brain lesions have been found to produce a variety of defects in speech and language (aphasia) involving both the understanding and production of speech and written and spoken language. Commonly, aphasics are unable to name objects or they misname them. In other cases remarkable defects in the ability to understand the meaning or significance of common objects (agnosia) have been found. It is common to find patients with parietal lobe lesions who neglect whole portions of their sensory spheres, including their own bodies, despite the fact that they seem to have normal sensation in those areas. For example, a parietal lobe patient may deny that his arm is his or may neglect to shave one side of his face and deny that it is there, despite the fact that stimulation of the arm or face shows fairly normal responsiveness.

Thus, the nervous system can be viewed as the machinery of information input to the organism, of information coding, and of the basic processes underlying sensation and perception. We know something of how response mechanisms are organized and controlled. And it is clear that motivation and emotion depend on the mutual interaction of the brain and the internal environment. The plasticity of the nervous system and the role of the brain in the adaptive processes of learning and memory are still too little understood. But we have gained some insight into the complexity of the brain mechanisms in memory and have made a start at unraveling their biochemistry.

Study of the brain has benefitted many patients who required surgery for tumors, treatment for epilepsy, or reeducation for aphasia. Many other direct benefits are in use or in prospect. One of the most interesting pursuits has been the use of computers to simulate brain functions. These highly imaginative exercises have resulted not only in a better understanding of the brain, but in improvement in computer technology as well.

3
MOTIVATION AND LEARNING

Perhaps the most persistent and difficult question in psychology concerns why a person thinks and acts the way he does. The heart of the question lies deeper than can be reached by any catalogue of what he knows, or what he is competent to do, or what options his life situation affords. The directive character of preferences, values, and attitudes, of physiological needs, personal volition, and social expectations comprises the subject matter that psychologists generally refer to as the study of motivation.

The importance of motivation for the management of behavior—our own and others'—is matched only by the importance of learning and habit. Indeed, these two psychological processes, motivation and learning, are so intimately linked that it is difficult to discuss one without the other. Our motives determine what lessons we will learn from experience, and the things we learn and remember are prime indicators of what will move us.

Motivation

Motivation, of course, is not a concern exclusively of psychologists. In addition to an enormous amount of common sense that our culture has accumulated about what people seek and what they avoid, about how to reward and punish them, about how to interest, persuade, discourage, or command them, there is a long history of philosophical discussion, a large body of economic theory, a well-developed system of managerial principles, a whole code of legal and adminstrative practices, and a growing knowledge of physiological mechanisms that are also concerned, directly or indirectly, with the nature of motivation.

The psychologist interested in problems of motivation may attack them in various ways. Laboratory studies of the effects of rewards on immediately preceding behavior have used many organisms, including man. Physiological states can be varied to observe effects on activity level and on the nature of activities. The use of symbolic rewards—tokens, buzzers, or lights, for example—aids in the understanding of the way in which motives are modified by prior experience. Comparison may be made of the backgrounds of highly motivated and less highly motivated humans and of the factors associated with observed differences. A large number of psychologists is employed in advertising and consumer research to assess the effects of major programs of persuasion through the mass media. By surveying attitudes, by analyzing production, or by generating experimental programs, psychologists in business and industry aid in developing and testing programs to increase productivity and in promoting healthy attitudes toward work of employees and management.

Rightly or wrongly every employer generates a program of rewards for work that employs motivational principles. Every parent faces the problem of choosing between reward and punishment in the control of children and in the development in them of the desirable motivations cherished by our society. Especially when our subtle programs of social control fail, as they do when college students riot, when workers engage in a slowdown, when the public refuses to buy an Edsel or to support an unpopular war, we question our understanding of the fundamental principles of motivation and behavior.

Ultimately, of course, we would like to know how to modify a person's motives, how to motivate children to want to learn more in school, how to motivate criminals to respect the law, how to relieve irrational motivations that afflict the neurotic and the insane, how to inspire a worker with a motive for achievement, how to strengthen the system of moral values and altruistic motives that support our society.

At the present time, however, our understanding of motivation is not sufficiently advanced to cause any great anxiety about its possible misuse. We should not, however, discount the rapid advances being made in psychopharmacology. Other fields of research are also contributing useful knowledge about human motivation. These studies include those dealing with such motives as man's need for achievement, for affiliation, and for power. Research on man's behavior as a consumer, voter and citizen, and as a worker or producer is also yielding new insights into human motivation and its influence on behavior. In addition, studies of organizations and how they motivate behavior as well as investigations of the dynamics of organizational change are gradually enriching our understanding of human motivation. Our present concern is to understand better how the existing methods for controlling motivation actually work.

Drives

The biological basis of motivation is most apparent in the case of those physiological systems essential for maintaining life and propagating the species. At this level man shares much with the other animals, and some recent advances in the physiological psychology of motivation are described elsewhere. Because physiological mechanisms seem somehow more substantial than thought or behavior, and because biological survival is a precondition for social adaptation, there have been many attempts to construct theories of social motivation based on our knowledge of the mechanisms involved in hunger, thirst, sex, pain, and other basic needs of the body. These drives possess an innate physiological basis. A baby is born with them and must have, or quickly acquire, means to satisfy them. It seems reasonable to consider, therefore, that other motivational patterns— desire for approval, curiosity, competence motivation, and the many agonistic and altruistic motives of adult humans—might somehow derive from, or be explained in terms of these essential biological motives.

Social Motives

One hypothesis proposes that social motives acquire their strength by repeated association with the satisfaction of biological drives. Social approval, for example, might become valuable because it is so often given or withheld in conjuction with giving or withholding food. Psychoanalytic theorists often account for social motives in terms of their association with the satisfaction of sexual urges. As plausible as such hypotheses may seem however, it has not been possible to verify them in careful studies of developing organisms. In many non-human species the social motives appear to have innate biological foundations of their own. Human socialization, the process of acquiring the social motives of one's society, certainly seem to be overlaid with symbolic processes that are connected only remotely, if at all, to physiological drives.

Many physiological drives can be described as homeostatic, that is, there is an optimal or satisfactory state that an organism attempts to maintain. A state of thirst, for example, normally indicates that the water balance in the tissue is upset, and drinking behavior returns the organism to homeostatic equilibrium. When an organism departs from its optimal state, signals are generated in the brain to activate behavior that will restore it. A great deal is known about such homeostatic mechanisms. An attractive hypothesis, therefore, is that this homeostatic principle might characterize all motivational states, social as well as biological. Here again, however, attempts to generalize directly from biological to social motives have met with little success. The need for social approval does not subside when approval is received. Men do not work for money only when their pockets are empty; a desire for money seems to grow by what it feeds on.

Indeed, the homeostatic principle does not even seem to describe all the innate physiological mechanisms that motivate behavior. The complexity of the problem is illustrated by aggressive behavior. When certain areas of the hypothalamus are stimulated electrically, spectacular outbursts of aggression can result. This is no blind reflex. The aggression is appropriately directed. Furthermore, such aggression has many of the properties of such drives as hunger or thirst. It can, like hunger or thirst, underlie the learning of new behavior. A cat stimulated in this way will learn to run through a T-maze to choose the one of two arms leading toward the goal box in which the rat to be attacked is confined. On those grounds, therefore, one would like to classify aggression as a drive state, yet it does not seem to involve some simple return to an optimal state of equilibrium.

If aggression is physiological drive, does that mean that all animals, man included, are unavoidably aggressive? Some theorists have argued that man's biological heritage makes aggression, violence, and war inevitable, but this argument overlooks the extent to which such behavior can be modified by learning. It is possible, for example, to train animals to be either unusually aggressive or unusually non-aggressive toward members of their own species. It is even possible to rear kittens with rats as playmates, and if the exposure occurs during a certain critical period in the kitten's development, it will grow up without any aggressive responses toward rats. In the light of such studies with animals, it is certainly premature to conclude that peace is incompatible with human nature. Obviously, we need to know a great deal more about the conditions that facilitate peaceful cooperation.

At the present time our understanding of the biological bases of human social motives is either slight or nonexistent. Energizing mechanisms must underlie social behavior, but they are modified by complex learning and symbolic processes that have so far eluded any precise physiological characterization.

Reinforcement

At a purely psychological level, however, there is much that can be learned about motivation even lacking any satisfactory theory of its physiological mechanisms. Perhaps the most intensive psychological research into the effects of motivation has been concerned with its intimate relation to the process of learning. The general observation that learning depends on motivation, that organisms learn to do those things that lead to satisfaction and to avoid behavior that has undesirable consequences, has inspired thousands of studies in psychological laboratories. The principle of reinforcement, which says that "rewarding" consequences of behavoir will tend to strengthen that behavior and lead to its reappearance on subsequent occasions, has been a key idea in many psychological theories, and it is frequently assumed (although it is not proved) that reinforcing consequences possess their power by virtue of their capacity to gratify the learner's motivational needs. A wide variety of organisms—birds, fish, rats, dogs, monkeys, man—will learn to push bars, run mazes, discriminate patterns, or operate machines if what they learn is associated with some reward, that is some reinforcing consequence. The principle is sufficiently general to hold across a wide range of biological species. The evolutionary advantages of being able to learn how to satisfy needs is obvious.

The management of learning by giving or withholding reinforcement has been studied in a variety of experimental situations. It is critically important in the classical Pavlovian conditioning experiment; it affects the learning of the adequate responses in mazes and puzzle boxes; it is perhaps most clearly the controlling factor in the sort of lever-pressing situation introduced by Skinner; and its effects can also be demonstrated in verbal learning and guessing experiments. It is not surprising therefore, that the principle of reinforcement has played a central role in most theories of learning, and that several mathematical formulations of this basic process have been developed to describe the changes that result in performance as a function of the reinforcement schedule.

Varying the reinforcement schedule can produce results that seem surprising on first encounter. For example, suppose that a hungry animal is given an opportunity to learn to push the lever in order to activate a mechanism that delivers a small pellet of food. If the mechanism delivers the food reinforcer on every press, a hungry rat will quickly learn to respond at a rate determined by its level of hunger and its rate of eating. If the mechanism is then deactivated, however, the lever-pressing behavior will soon stop, it will be extinguished. As measured by this extinction procedure, the response established by regular reinforcement will not be particularly strong or persistent. Now what will happen if the reinforcement is not regular but is delivered only some of the times that the lever is pushed? The rat still learns, but the strength of its response can be defined as being greater than with regular reinforcement since the behavior will occur more rapidly and will be more resistant to extinction. There is a simple, direct relationship between the amount of work done and the amount of reinforcement received.

B. F. Skinner and his associates have investigated a wide range of reinforcement schedules. By using small, special purpose computers to control the contingencies between response and reinforcement it is possible to study the effects of giving reinforcement after fixed or variable numbers of responses, or after fixed or variable intervals of time, or only for responses occurring within some schedule for paced responses. Experiments of this type have provided sensitive techniques for the analysis of behavior. These techniques can be used to study the normal development of learning and motivation, of course, but they can also be used to study the disruptive effects of emotion, drugs, brain damage, and other physiological manipulations of the nervous system.

The effects of reinforcement on learning have been studied with human as well as animal subjects. Indeed, Skinner has made his research on animals the basis for his theories of programmed instruction, with results that have opened new lines of advance in educational psychology. In man, however, our capacity for complex symbolic processes vastly complicates the picture of reinforcement seen in animal studies. Indeed, with human learners it often seems that knowledge of results, the symbolic recognition of success or failure, is more important than the actual reinforcing stimulus itself. Moreover, human beings seem to be able to take on, or internalize, the role of the reinforcing agent. This ability to reinforce ourselves symbolically is extremely important in determining our social behavior.

Academic Motivation

Consider, for example, the problem of motivating children to do well in their school work. The importance of this problem is dramatically illustrated by the now well-documented finding that at all grade levels, and in all regions of the country, black children are about one standard deviation below white on achievement tests. (Such a difference means that only 16 percent of one group is above the average of the other group.) This fact is sometimes cited to prove the innate superiority of Caucasians, but the explanation may have much less to do with innate differences in intelligence than with matters of motivation. Black children typically are not interested in school work. How much a child achieves is affected by how much he studies, and that, in turn, depends on how much he is motivated.

Various hypotheses have been advanced to explain why black children are not motivated to learn in academic situations. Some theorists blame the parents for failing to recognize and support academic motivation in their children. Others claim that a ghetto environment deprives black children of the stimulation necessary for cognitive growth. Others blame our schools for being irrelevant to the black child's motivations. Still others blame teachers for fostering antiacademic attitudes through poor pedagogic practices. Without deciding whether any or all of these suggestions are correct, the fact seems to be that in our American society many black children are sent to school without having acquired the kind of orientation that is basic to effective academic motivation. They are less inclined to make the self-reinforcing responses to their own performance which sustain most children from a middle-class environment.

If this is in fact the situation in our schools, we can attack it through programs developed on the basis of adequate research. For example, Negro boys were selected on the basis of teachers' ratings as being among the most successful or least successful fifth and sixth graders in a predominantly black school. They were given a series of simple tasks to perform and were asked to evaluate how well they had performed upon completion of each task. It was found that boys who were academically unsuccessful engaged in significantly more self-criticism and were significantly less favorable in their self-evaluation, even though independent judges could perceive no objective inferiority in the quality of their work. Moreover, the unsuccessful boys reported more instances of negative reinforcement at home and showed significantly more anxiety. The children who were doing poorly in school had, in a sense, learned to impose failure upon themselves. Their situation was aggravated by the fact that the same children who think so little of their own performance frequently hold aspirations for academic accomplishment and advanced study that are as high as or higher than their more successful peers'. This combination of high aspirations and low self-esteem can contribute to growing anxiety and demoralization. It is not necessary to instill higher standards in these children in order to motivate them. What seems to be needed is a more supportive environment that would teach them to place a higher value on their own abilities and performance and that would enable them to develop the self-reinforcing mechanisms that can make hard study seem rewarding.

Social reinforcement phenomena are exceedingly complex, of course, but we must learn more about how self-reinforcing responses to one's performances are acquired through experiences of approval and disapproval by adults. It is not only a problem of great interest for psychological theory, but one that seems to be essential for understanding the widespread academic failure of socially underprivileged children in the United States.

Self-Consistency as a Motive

The question of whether one holds an accurate appraisal of one's own abilities is a special case of a more general class of motivation that is extremely important in influencing human behavior. There is considerable evidence that most people place a very high value on knowing in general whether their opinions and beliefs are correct. In order to obtain such verification they must compare themselves with other people, and much social contact is so motivated. Moreover, they want to have consistent information, consistent with their own beliefs and prior knowledge, or information that at least seems consistent to them. If the information they have appears inconsistent, they will be motivated to make it consistent by either changing their behavior or the way they think about it, or by collecting new information and new opinions.

Consider a situation in which several mutually exclusive alternatives, all more or less attractive, are available to a person who is forced to choose among them, and suppose that the decision will have important consequences for him. Each alternative has certain features in its favor, but once a decision is made in favor of one of them, the person may, in order to support his belief that he has made the best (right) choice, persuade himself that the other alternatives were really less attractive than they previously seemed. A student who chooses one college out of several alternatives, for example, will soon persuade himself that his college is really much better than the others.

The desire for consistency as a pervasive motive in human affairs has played a role in numerous psychological theories. In psycho-analytic theory, for example, the process is called rationalization. Experiences of inconsistency are not restricted to choice situations, of course. It is inconsistent with one's conception of a friend to see him cheat. It is inconsistent with one's conception of himself as father to learn that his son has stolen money. It is inconsistent with one's conception of himself to learn that someone he respects thinks he has shown poor judgment. In such situations people are strongly motivated to resolve the inconsistency, to change their behavior, opinions, feelings, or sources of information. At this level of gener-ality, the motivation that guides human behavior is highly symbolic and its underlying mechanisms are part and parcel of our general cognitive systems for gathering, evaluating, and using information about ourselves and the world in which we live.

Motivation in Employment

In recent years modern management practices have given increas-ing attention to problems of motivation of employees. In a variety of industrial settings production has been substantially increased by a mixture of practices that places emphasis on human relations, on communication, and on employee involvement in decisions rather than relying solely on pay and related extrinsic rewards. The imagi-native programs of many industries suggest ways in which schools and communities might improve their practices in motivating indi-viduals and groups.

4
COLLECTING AND ANA-
LYZING INFORMATION

Psychologists have always been deeply interested in the way in which man perceives the world around him, and the way in which information collected by the sense organs is analyzed and made meaningful. The apparently simple process of seeing color requires a highly complex sensing system as yet not well understood. The almost magical way in which the eye increases in sensitivity in darkness challenges man to understand the process. The highly sensitive vestibular apparatus that helps us maintain balance and causes severe nausea and disorganization when disturbed had to be fully understood prior to exposing men to space flight experiences.

Historically, the study of sensory processes is the oldest branch of scientific psychology. The philosophy of British empiricism in the eighteenth century emphasized the importance of sensory experience in the growth of the mind, and the sensory physiology of nineteenth-century Germany provided a solid base for interpreting sensory phenomena in terms of the anatomy and physiology of the receptor systems. Today the senses are no longer regarded as the "windows of the soul," but the study of sensation and perception still holds a central place in psychological research.

Detection and Discrimination

Much research on sensory psychology is concerned with thresholds, with the measurement of the smallest energies to which receptors are sensitive, or the smallest differences that they can resolve. Over the years many methods for making such measurements have been developed, standards for normal performance have been established, and physical and chemical explanations for receptor processes have been advanced. This research, which is a central topic of the field that is called *psychophysics*, has accumulated to the point where it is now probably the best understood area in the whole domain of psychology.

A sensory threshold is not an all-or-none affair. As the stimulus energy decreases toward zero, or as a difference between two stimuli is progressively diminished, there is no point at which we suddenly stop being affected by it. Instead, as the threshold is approached there is progressive decline in the probability that the stimulus, or stimulus-difference, will be correctly detected. This statistical character of the threshold has led psychophysicists to borrow from electrical engineers the concept of the receiver operating characteristic (ROC curve). Any detection device—including, apparently, the human being—can be "set" to report signals at different levels of probability. If it is important to detect everything and if false reports are not expensive, the criterion for reporting can be set quite low. If, on the contrary, false reports are expensive and missed signals are unimportant, the criterion can be set quite high. There is a necessary trade off between misses and false reports; for any detection device there is a limit to how far we can go in eliminating both kinds of error. The discovery of this trading relation has enabled psychophysicists to understand relations among threshold measurements made under different conditions and different instructions, or different consequences of detection. By changing instructions, different sensitivities can be obtained for observers assigned to any particular detection task, a point of considerable importance in a variety of inspection and surveillance systems.

Interpretation

Detection and discrimination are only the beginning of the perceptual process. A stimulus (or stimulus difference) must be interpreted by being related to ongoing activities. Perhaps the simplest interpretation by the perceiver is the magnitude or qualitative nature of the stimulus (or stimulus difference). Beyond such elementary estimations are problems of recognition and naming, of fitting the stimulus event into a spatio-temporal context provided by other stimuli, or of assigning values or other symbolic significance to the sensory event. These interpretive processes, and the neurophysiological mechanisms underlying them, constitute the core of perceptual psychology. From the great variety of investigations of these interpretive processes a few examples are mentioned.

Subjective Scaling

Not only can we detect the occurrence of a tone, but we can say something about its loudness, its pitch, its duration. Lights are not merely on or off; lights have brightness, color, size, shape, and duration, and they can be referred to a spatial location, near or far, left or right, up or down. We are sensitive to a wide range of light energies, and it is possible for observers to estimate reliably where in this range a visual event lies.

It is important to distinguish between subjective properties of a sensory event and the physical properties of the stimulus. We can, of course, measure the intensity of an acoustic stimulus, but there is no simple, direct relation between this physical quantity and how loud a person will say it was. The subjective estimate is related to the physical quantity, but is not identical with it. An increase in intensity of a soft noise will seem much greater, for example, than the same increase in a loud noise. The relationship between the physical event and the subject report can be stated quite precisely, through a wide range of stimulus intensities, and for different sense modalities.

Studies of subjective scaling have significance far beyond the sensory and perceptual processes for which they were first developed. Methods invented and refined in the psychophysical laboratory have repeatedly been applied to problems such as the measurement of attitudes, expectations, meanings, and other complex psychological phenomena. Even though there is no objective external reference against which these subjective scales can be compared, subjective scaling can be performed dependably (reliably) to yield estimates of the strength or magnitude of these highly subjective states.

Recognition

Many problems of recognition—identifying which of several possibilities the stimulus happens to be—can be characterized most conveniently in terms of the theory of selective information developed for communication engineering. The amount of information that a signal contains is not determined by the physical properties of the signal itself, but by the size of the set of alternatives from which it was chosen. If a signal is constant, it conveys no information; if it is one of two equally probable alternatives, it conveys one "bit" of information. Four equiprobable alternatives contain two bits, eight contain three, etc. The number of bits of information that must be received in order to correctly identify one of N equiprobable stimuli is $\log N$. This measure, developed in order to quantify the concept of channel capacity in general, can be applied to humans as well as to machines.

For example, suppose that tones of different frequencies are to be recognized. When only three or four different tones are used, little confusion results, but as the number of alternatives increases, most listeners (those not blessed with absolute pitch) begin to make more and more mistakes. Channel capacity is sufficient to support errorless recognition of about 4 to 6 different frequencies of vibration; beyond that we cannot go without rapidly rising error rates.

In a variety of recognition tasks involving simple stimuli of this kind our channel capacity turns out to be in the general neighborhood of 5 to 10 alternatives. How can this rather poor performance be reconciled with the fact that we are able to recognize hundreds or thousands of faces, objects, pieces of music, or foods? The reason is that these stimuli are multidimensional, they differ from one another in many ways, whereas simple stimuli differ from one another along a single dimension, like pitch, loudness, brightness, or length. If we add a second dimension to a stimulus—varying the tones in both frequency and amplitude, for example—the channel capacity goes up. If, as seems to be the case, we can resolve 2.5 bits of information about frequency and 2 bits about loudness, then one might logically expect that we would be able to transmit 4.5 bits about the two together. In fact, however, the addition is not perfect. The experimental result is about 3.5 bits. As we add more dimensions the channel capacity continues to increase, but at a decreasing rate. When stimuli vary along a large number of different dimensions, it seems that we can ordinarily discriminate approximately one bit of information (present or absent) about each dimension.

Not all the psychological problems of recognition can be reduced to this form, of course. There are many puzzles involved in the development of recognition skills, in the effects of drugs or brain injury on performance, and in the availability of the identifying response after recognition has occurred. Many psychologists work not merely to understand these phenomena but also to aid in programs to improve sensory experience and perception.

The Gestalt

The term *Gestalt* was introduced into the American vocabulary by a distinguished group of German psychologists who fled Hitler during the 1930s but brought their language with them. These men emphasized the role of organization, form, configuration (Gestalt), and modeled many of their ideas after the field theories of physics. Their best examples were cases of perceptual organization, although they extended the argument into every branch of psychological science.

Perhaps the most basic principle advanced by Gestalt psychologists is the organization of the perceptual field into figure and ground. To a certain extent the selection of the figure is under voluntary control, as it is when we listen selectively to one instrument or another during a symphony. But there is only one figure at a time, and what it can be is strongly influenced by relations among the parts of the field. When we look at an object we see it—the nervous system is designed to organize it—as a clear, coherent, organized whole, set off from, but located in terms of, the extraneous surroundings. We see the objects around us, and not the space between them, although the pattern of energies that falls on our retinas presents as much information about the spaces as about the objects. How this figure and ground organization is achieved is not some simple matter we can take for granted. Its complexity can perhaps be appreciated by trying to imagine what kind of machine we would have to add to a camera so that it would draw a clear contour around the objects in any picture it took.

It is easier to organize the figure, of course, if it is spatially continuous, but spatial continuity is not essential. It is also possible to see a group of objects as the figure. In such cases it is necessary for the separate parts to be related in certain ways, or share certain properties. Among the factors that affect grouping are proximity, similarity, common fate (if they move together at the same time in the same direction), directional continuity, closure (if they produce a closed, stable, balanced, or symmetrical figure), habit, and the set or attitude of the perceiver. These factors can be translated into manipulable variables in perceptual experiments, where the influence of one is pitted against or added to the influence of others, and where observers are asked to report on the phenomenological Gestalt that results.

The lesson of Gestalt psychology is that our perception of an object is not a passive registration of the physical stimuli representing that object, but depends in highly complex and predictable ways on relations among all parts of the perceptual field. Psychological theory has not yet explained all the configurational phenomena that Gestalt psychologists have pointed out, but no serious attempt to account for the facts of perception can afford to ignore them.

Guiding and Response

In addition to detection and interpretation, perception plays a critical role in our ability to control our own behavior. When we reach for an object, our perception of the discrepancy between the position of the object and the position of our hand guides the movement so that the discrepancy is progressively reduced. The stimulus information is organized to facilitate the response, and many of the phenomena of perception are intelligible only in terms of this guidance function.

The importance of perceptual feedback is most dramatically illustrated when people wear special goggles with prisms that displace, or even completely invert, the visual field. At first the distorting lenses cause incoordination, laborious movement, apparent swinging of the visual field as the head is moved, and so on. After a few days of continuous experience, however, all this is suppressed. A whole new set of visual and motor relations is learned, until ultimately the distorted world becomes a familiar place. Even an inverted visual world will no longer seem to be upside down. It is significant that complete adaptation requires active movement, walking, and the use of the hands and legs in the visual field. If the same period of time were spent being moved about passively in a wheelchair, little or no adaptation would ensue. Visual and motor coordination involves building up a store of correlations between self-produced movements and their perceptual consequences. Passive use of the eyes alone is not sufficient.

Space Perception

Because behavior occurs in a three-dimensional world, perceptual information is organized in spatial coordinates. Since the retinal image is a two-dimensional display, the question of how the brain constructs the three-dimensional environment from this retinal information has always been a central problem of perceptual theory.

Psychologists have devised ingenious devices to test the degree to which the observer will misperceive the nature of a visual field in order to make it fit into his normal experience. These demonstrations make it clear that the perceiver is at least as important as the stimulus in determining what is perceived. As we conjecture about the next unusual experiences of astronauts we can see the necessity for considerable training to avoid the hazards of serious misperceptions in the strange surroundings of outer space.

Consider the patterns of reflected light that are formed when objects are illuminated in the ordinary way. The world we look at consists mostly of surfaces at various angles and in various relations to one another, and it is the organization of these surfaces that is the principal task of space perception. For example, surfaces generally have some kind of texture—grain, weave, stippling, waves, etc. —so that if a surface slants away from the observer, its texture will appear to change, with finer texture in the distance. This texture gradient provides information about the spatial orientation of the surface. There are several such sources of information about spatial relations. There is information about space in the difference between the images formed on the two retinas. There is linear perspective, interposition, shadow, and so on.

The real complexity of space perception only becomes apparent, however, when we consider the effects of motion either by the object perceived or by the perceiver himself. For example, when a familiar object approaches us there is a regular increase in the size of its optical image on the retina. However, we do not see the object as increasing in size; we see it increase in proximity. This phenomenon, called size constancy, implies that the apparent size of an object is determined by information from the entire visual field, that our perception depends on the relation of the object to all the other features that provide the spatial coordinates of our visual world.

Consider what happens when we change our point of fixation. As we move our eyes from left to right, the image cast on the retina moves rapidly from right to left. But we do not see the world around us swinging this way and that every time we change our point of regard. Instead, we see a stable environment, and refer the changes to our own movements. Conversely, if we maintain a steady fixation and the object moves, its movement does not blur our perception of it. Instead, its motion often serves to clarify its location and orientation. The distortions in the fluidly changing retinal image of moving, rotating objects provide information that we use in order to construct a perception of a rigid object.

Attention, Perception, and Memory

Sudden and unexpected changes in the pattern of stimulation have the power to control attention, to shift our attention to the unexpected event. There is a kind of heightened clarity about the perceptual processes that are at the focus of attention. We know that, although attention can be shifted quite rapidly, we cannot pay attention simultaneously to two or more different things. We have even been able to record changes in the sensory nervous input to the brain as a function of shifts in an animal's focus of perception.

Attention is a selective process that goes on in time, of course; and normally a clear perceptual focus on some object or event will make it possible to perform further operations on it, to name it, form associations to it, rehearse the response to it, transfer the information into some more permanent form of storage, and so on. One hypothesis, previously described, that is currently motivating considerable psychological research is that several stages can be experimentally distinguished. There is first some kind of sensory process; next, attention focuses perception on a part of the sensory input; then the information is available in short-term memory for several seconds, during which time it may be further attended to; and if the information is kept in attention over a long period of time, there is a measurable probability that it will be transferred into a long-term store where it can be recognized or recalled for use at some later time. It is possible to devise experimental situations in which a person's performance at these successive stages is either interrupted or directed along particular channels, and to measure the accuracy and latency of his responses to various kinds of test questions. This line of research should help us optimize people's acquisition of information in situations of widely varying kinds—in man and machine interactions, in educational situations, in tasks of skill or sport—and to diagnose the sources of difficulty when, for one reason or another, a person fails to perform as well as we think he should.

In summary, a long history of research on how we collect and analyze information about ourselves and the world in which we live shows that perception is no simple process of passive registration. Sensory information is detected, organized, recognized, represented, and attended to in a form suitable to guide the adaptive behavior of the organism. How this is done is one of the most complex, mysterious, and important problems in the whole domain of psychology.

5

LANGUAGE AND THINKING

Man differs from other animals most spectacularly by his possession of language. The evolution of a capacity for verbal symbolization has produced improvements in communication and thinking that have set the human species apart. A concern for the psychological implications of this remarkable competence has always played a central role in the efforts of psychologists to understand the mind and behavior of human beings.

In one way or another, nearly every line of research in human psychology has some contribution to make to our understanding of how people acquire or use language. The study of perception, for example, includes the study of speech perception. Developmental psychologists trace the child's acquisition of language. Social psychology is concerned with verbal beliefs and processes of persuasion. Clinical psychology uses verbal methods of therapy. The study of learning includes the learning of verbal materials. The study of thinking and reasoning is intimately enmeshed in the verbal representation of thoughts and reasons. Intelligence tests measure vocabulary size. Wherever we turn, the effects of language on human thought and behavior are manifest. The following is but a sample of the ways psychologists have investigated this ubiquitous phenomenon.

Language

Formally, a language can be defined as the set of grammatical sentences that can be formed on a given vocabulary. Functionally, a language is a means of communication among the members of a social group. For a psychologist it is not enough to have a grammatical description of the rules that characterize grammatical sentences. He is concerned with performance, with actual usage. He wants to know how the rules of language are acquired, what cognitive mechanisms underlie the production and interpretation of actual utterances, what consequences these mechanisms have for personal thought and social cooperation. The psychological description of a language user must include the description of his language, but it cannot end there. These problems have provided the core of a rapidly developing branch of psychology called psycholinguistics.

Verbal Learning

Broadly conceived, the study of verbal learning is concerned with how people extract and remember information they receive in verbal messages. This learning depends on many conditions—on the prior knowledge and beliefs of the learner, on his aptitude, interest, and motivation, on the form in which the information is presented and the source from which it comes, on the time he devotes to it and the uses to which he puts it. Thus, any experimental study of verbal learning is forced to concentrate on particular features and to select a few to incorporate into experimental tasks in such a way that precise information on performance can be obtained. Consequently, most research in this field appears considerably narrower than the broad conception psychologists hold of its ultimate goal.

For example, one process of central importance for any kind of verbal learning is the formation of associations. Words are associated with one another, names are associated with their referents, sentences are associated with their meanings. Long before psychology became experimental, the philosophers had emphasized the importance of association. It is a natural strategy, therefore, to try to isolate this process from all else that may be going on in verbal learning and to discover the laws that govern it.

In order to study association in its purest form, one would like to have verbal materials that were uncontaminated by previous learning. With adult learners this goal seems unobtainable; but it can be approached, as Ebbinghaus proposed in 1885, by using nonsense syllables, for example, FAP, GUJ, QOW, etc. The technique Ebbinghaus introduced, which has been followed in hundreds of subsequent experiments, is to require the learner to memorize nonsense materials and to measure his mastery in terms of the number of items he can recall. Rote memorization has been carefully plotted as a function of the amount of material to be learned, the nature and amount of practice, the conditions of reinforcement, and the age, intelligence, and prior experience of the learner. The major factors affecting performance on such tasks are now reasonably well understood and theoretical formulations have become increasingly explicit, even to the point of mathematical formalization.

Consider, for example, the length of the list to be learned. If it contains only five nonsense syllables, an experienced subject will be able to repeat them in the correct order after a single presentation. One might expect, therefore, that he could repeat ten correctly after two presentations, fifteen after three, and so forth; but this is not generally the case. Apparently the process of holding the first five syllables in memory somehow interferes with acquisition of a second five. Analysis of errors indicates that it is the middle of the list (or just past the middle) that is most difficult; this "serial-position effect" has received much experimental attention since it is a feature that any theory of rote memorization must take into account.

Even in this simple experiment we see the effects of interference. Apparently associations are not formed in a psychological vacuum; the formation of one association is influenced by the other associations we are trying to form at the same time. If, therefore, we shift our attention from the problem of how associations are formed to the problem of how they are dissolved, these interference effects will play a central role. One theory holds that forgetting is not a passive process of decay, but is the result of active interference with old associations when we try to establish new ones. The interference theory of forgetting has been the subject of many experimental studies.

Even the most meaningless verbal materials will not completely frustrate a learner's effort to find sense in them. If the nonsense syllables can be related to something the learner already knows, he can bring to bear his previous learning to facilitate his performance.

Instead of forming a new association between FAP and GUJ, and then another between GUJ and QOW, many learners will instead remember something like "Fat Gus quit," and introduce corrections to recover the nonsense syllables. These recording strategies make the learning process quite different from the simple formation of new associations. In recent work, therefore, more attention has been paid to the learner's effort after meaning, and materials have been designed to study what makes material meaningful and how meaning operates to facilitate new learning.

It is impossible in a few short paragraphs to do justice to the ingenuity and perseverance of the scientists who have attacked these basic questions in the theory of associative learning. Methods of experimentation have been refined, quantification has been precise and reliable, theories have been explicit and quantitative. Yet the results are still far short of a general theory of verbal learning, broadly conceived. In particular, the conditions that optimize rote memorization in the laboratory do not seem particularly relevant or helpful for the kind of verbal learning that goes on in the classroom. In the more general situation, of course, the serious student is not merely memorizing. He thinks about what he is learning, he concentrates more on the difficult parts, he translates the information into his own words and tries to relate it to some previously established system of concepts. This thinking, evaluating, translating, relating activity is not easily measurable in quantitative terms. In spite of excellent progress to date, we still have much to learn about the conditions that facilitate or impede verbal learning.

Short-Term Verbal Memory

If, in the course of a rote memorization experiment, one were to interrupt the procedure at some point and ask the learner what he had just seen, he would nearly always be able to respond correctly. If he perceives the syllable or word correctly, he can hold it at least momentarily in short-term memory. But in the normal course of events it may drop out very rapidly and be unavailable when recall is tested later.

If a person is given a single nonsense syllable, like GQF, and then immediately distracted by some such task as counting backward by threes from 782, by the time 20 seconds have passed his probability of correct recall will have dropped to 0.2. This rapid fading of short-term memory does not occur if there is only one trial. The first time he tries it, a person will have a probability of success of about 0.8. But inhibition builds up very rapidly, and by the fourth trial he will find it very difficult indeed. If on the fifth trial he is given three numbers instead of three letters, his performance will jump back up to 0.8; changing the type of materials used will produce a sudden release from inhibition. There seem to be interference effects that are quite specific to the particular class of materials remembered.

The specificity of such materials is also demonstrated by the fact that TQRM2326 is easier to recall after a single presentation than is T2Q3R2M6. Moreover, the alternating list is far more difficult at rapid rates of presentation; at slow rates the learner has time to shift his attention from one universe to the other.

Recall of Sentences

The complex information processing that occurs in short-term memory is dramatically illustrated in the interpretation and recall of grammatical sentences. Even the simplest sentences, "The boy ate the apple," are not processed the way we process a string of unrelated words, "apple the ate boy the." We recognize the meanings of the words, group them into phrases, identify the subject, verb, and object, and assign an interpretation to the whole complex structure. The rapid processes by which this is accomplished are highly overlearned through years of usage, which makes their detailed analysis an extremely challenging problem for psycholinguistics.

For more complex sentences, the problem is correspondingly more difficult. Apparently simple, active, declarative, affirmative sentences are easiest to understand and remember. If we form the passive, the interrogative, or the negative, additional processing is required. In recall tests it is found that people often remember the underlying propositional content, but forget some of the gramatical transforma-tions that were applied to it. "Wasn't the apple eaten by the boy," for example, may be recalled as "Didn't the boy eat the apple" or "The apple was eaten by the boy," that is, with some of the transformations deleted. Other things being constant, people try to dig out the base structure of the sentence, the form that is most simple in semantic interpretation. They remember this semantic interpretation, then later try to reconstruct the precise syntactic form in which the idea was presented.

Still more complex sentences result when simple sentences are compounded into longer ones. For example, there are grammatical transformations that combine the underlying structures of "The boy was hungry" and "The boy ate the apple" to give "The boy who was hungry ate the apple," or "The hungry boy ate the apple" or "The apple was what the boy who was hungry ate," and so on. Here again our effort seems to be to recover the underlying propositional content. Long sentences are, of course, harder to remember than short ones, and the reason seems to be that long sentences generally contain more simple subject and predicate components.

Psycholinguistic studies of memory for sentences have given us a picture of the way in which our short-term memory holds the input long enough to extract and interpret the base components as they appear successively in the sentence. This information is rapidly transferred to some growing conception of what the message is saying, thus making room in short-term memory for the next phrase or clause. Precisely how this is done is still unknown, but it is obvious that many of the surface details of phrasing and expression are lost in the development of this underlying conception of the content of the message. As we learn more about sentence processing, however, the application of results from the psychological laboratory to the practical situations of everyday learning should prove increasingly possible.

Thought and Inner Speech

Which of the following four words does not belong with the other three?

ADD   SUBTRACT   MULTIPLY   INCREASE

Most people say that increase does not belong. Problems of this sort are often used in psychological tests; they test both a person's vocabulary and his ability to see abstract similarities. However, this particular instance would not be a good test item, because two of the words—add and multiply can be used in more than one context. For example, if the same four words are written in a different order:

ADD   INCREASE   MULTIPLY   SUBTRACT

most people say that subtract does not belong.

This simple fact tells us something about the way people think. As words are read from left to right, a concept develops in such a way that, wherever possible, successive words modify rather than replace it. This modify-rather-than-replace strategy for processing information—sometimes called a "focussing" strategy—is deeply ingrained in us. The result of applying it here is that we judge the second unambiguous word to be inappropriate more often than the first. Which illustrates one of the innumerable ways that talking and thinking intertwine.

At least since Plato's well-known remark that thought is the soul's conversation with itself, men have puzzled over the relation of thought and language. Is thinking just speech without sound? Or are thought and language completely unrelated? No single, simple answer suffices.

The first notion to dispense with is that thought is nothing more than inner speech. Under certain conditions, thought may involve inner speech, but there is little reason to believe the two are identical. Studies of animal behavior show convincingly that animals are capable of insightful problem solving. Apes are particularly intelligent. Chimpanzees, for example, have been seen to use tools, and even to manufacture tools for special purposes—all without anything like a language to think with. Or consider studies of deaf children. Congenital deafness inevitably delays language development, yet the capacity for conceptual thinking is not correspondingly impaired. Moreover, injuries to the language areas in the brain do not reduce their unfortunate victims to mental incompetence. On the contrary, aphasic patients seem to retain much if not all of their intellectual competence in spite of their language disorder. Thought, therefore, cannot be defined as a particular kind of subvocal speech, since much, if not all, thought can proceed in the absence of linguistic abilities.

Consider the opposite extreme. Is it possible that thought and language are completely independent, as unrelated say, as digestion and walking? Could it be sheer coincidence that man, the talking animal, happens to have rational powers unequaled elsewhere in the animal kingdom? Once again, clinical evidence is helpful. Although speech may be impaired without affecting thought, the reverse does not seem to be true. When our capacity to think is affected—by alcohol, insanity, fatigue, damage to the brain, or in any other way— it reflects directly in our speech. So we cannot say that speaking and thinking are unrelated. Too many of the problems we think about would not exist if they could not be phrased in words. Thus the riddle begins to emerge. Thought and language are neither identical nor independent. Some more complicated relation must be sought.

One relevant observation is the following: A problem may be easier when it is posed in one language than in another. The thinking of people who speak very different languages has been studied, but such comparisons are difficult to make with any precision. Natural languages are rich in alternative ways to formulate any given problem, and translations are hard to evaluate. The point can be made more clearly with artificial languages, such as mathematics. Why, for example, is it so much easier to do long division in Arabic than in Roman notation for the numbers? The concepts involved are the same; only the symbols differ. And yet the mind runs far more smoothly in one case than the other. There are at least two reasons for this kind of interaction between language and thinking. One, we know the Arabic system much better. We have had more practice with it. But that fact alone is not sufficient to explain the effect. Another factor is also at work, namely, the Arabic system fits the conceptual structure of the problem more adequately. To develop particular examples, however, would lead us into more detail than we can afford.

Problem-Solving

In order to obtain data on the more subtle uses of symbolism in thought and learning, psychologists often ask people to "think out loud" as they work on a problem. The monologue that results is a running description of what the thinker was doing. Such accounts are convenient, of course, but they can also be misleading. Too much of what we call thinking occurs somewhere outside of consciousness and is not available for introspective observation, and too much more is colored by personal desires and defenses. A thinker's verbal report, therefore, has the status of a hypothesis, not a fact; further tests are needed before it can be accepted.

In complicated cases—analyzing a chess position, say, or finding a logical proof—a thinker's account of his train of thought may be so extensive and entail such a complex variety of assumptions and strategies that it becomes difficult to understand, much less to verify, the implications of what he says he is doing. Suppose a thinker's description suggests to us that he is proceeding with certain priorities according to certain simple rules, but that there are enough rules and their interactions are sufficiently intricate to baffle intuitive analysis. In that case a psychologist may try to be completely explicit. He may write out precisely what he thinks the rules are, specifying the order in which they are to be tried, the conditions under which they apply, and the consequences of applying them. His goal is to state the rules in such a way that anyone who followed them would be led through exactly the same sequence of questions and answers about the problem as were reported in the thinker's original protocol. Once such a set of rules has been formulated, the theorist must painstakingly test it for a range of problems and for variations in its several parameters. This is one direction that research has taken in this field in recent years.

The tedium of evaluating the implications of a complex system of rules can be enormously reduced by the use of high-speed digital computers. Psychologists and others have developed programs specially designed for such work—for listing objects, properties, and relations, and for characterizing the operations that rules entail—so that a psychological hypothesis can be effectively translated into a computer program that will (if the hypothesis is not incorrect) cause the machine to simulate what a human being does. Computer simulation has enabled psychologists to study theories and hypotheses that are far more complicated than anyone would have dared to tackle only two or three decades ago. Information-processing models have led to a revitalization of interest in and research on the venerable and hitherto intractable problems of thinking.

A complex system of rules that characterizes a thinker's performance, and that provides the basis for programming a computer to simulate that performance effectively comprises a theory of that particular type of thinking in much the same sense that a system of differential equations might comprise a theory of some physical process. Theories formulated in terms of rules rather than laws are, of course, quite common in the behavioral and social sciences. There need be no normative implication that it is "good" to follow the rule and "bad" or "illegal" to violate it; in the scientific context a rule is a purely descriptive summary of the behavior that has been observed. Indeed, a person who obeys a rule, whose behavior conforms to it, may not himself be able to state that rule explicitly. Probably the most intricate systems of implicit rules regulating human behavior are the rules of language.

Creativity

One criticism that has been made of the effort to formulate a theory of thinking in terms of a system of rules is that such a thinker could not be truly creative. If that were the way people thought, then nothing new, nothing not already implicit in the rules, could ever occur. This criticism is difficult to evaluate, largely because we are so unclear about the differences between creative and noncreative thinking. If "creative" is, as some believe, an adjective we apply to activities that seem both useful and surprising, then it is easy to display instances of creativity by machines, as in the use of computers to develop new words for use as trade names. Satisfactory resolution of this issue must await a better definition of creativity.

Psychologists have devoted much attention to originality and creativity. Experts have designated people who have made creative contributions to various fields and psychologists have tested them extensively to uncover the nature and source of their special gifts. Creative people are generally above average in intelligence, and they seem to rely on that intelligence to put the pieces back together in a novel way after they have analyzed a problem into its essentials. Indeed, a capacity to tolerate the near chaos that results after traditional modes of thought have been abandoned and before novel modes have replaced them has often led ordinary people to suspect that something was psychologically odd about their creative acquaintances.

Discussions of creativity almost necessarily have a metaphorical quality. We can frequently recognize creativity, but we cannot predict or control it. It would be of great social value if we knew how to create creativity—if, for example, we could train people to be original. Some attempts have been made in this direction. People have been given the same word association test repeatedly, along with the instruction that they must give a new response every time. The first time the test is given, the word "chair," say, may make them respond "table," but the second time through they have to give a different response to "chair," and the third time still another, and so on. This training (which quickly becomes surprisingly frustrating) will generalize to other similar tasks, for example, thinking of unusual uses for common objects. But whether this kind of "originality training" has practical consequences outside of the training situation remains an unanswered question.

At present, research on creativity remains in an uncertain state. The problem is obviously important, many people have proposed interesting hypotheses about it, some empirical studies have turned up suggestive evidence, and much worthwhile work is under way. But unless the problem can be more clearly defined, it will be difficult to recognize a solution when we see one. Meanwhile, there is much to be learned about simpler cognitive processes, where progress is perhaps less consequential but certainly more assured.

6
THE GROWING CHILD

Perhaps at no previous time in the history of man has a society addressed itself so earnestly to questions about the proper upbringing of children. People are concerned about the adequacy of the intellectual experiences of disadvantaged children, distressed about the apparent later effects of early permissiveness in child rearing, and outraged at the crime and violence of those who have not been adequately "socialized," those who have failed to learn to respond to the subtle ways in which a society enforces its standards of conduct.

The growing interest in the child has been reflected in the expanding numbers of psychologists who work in this domain and in the substantial increase in the amount of support for research and programs of community action and education. A notable example is the National Institute of Child Health and Human Development.

Traditionally, psychologists have directed major attention to various aspects of human development. The systematic study of children was part of the response of scientists to Darwin's proposals on the ancestry of man. Darwin and his followers saw the child as a natural laboratory for the study of development; evolutionary changes in the species and changes in man as a member of emerging civilized society might be seen reflected in the growth of the child's body and mind. G. Stanley Hall, Founder of the American Psychological Association, was the evangelist of child study in the United States. Hall influenced the profession with his students and with his commitment to the scientific study of the child as a mirror of man evolving. Psychologists soon lost respect for the analogy between the evolution of species and the development of the child; but by then a foundation had been established for the disciplined study of the growing mind.

Developmental psychology has been organized around two major themes. A precise description has been sought for the regular changes in behavior that take place as the child grows—the normative problem—and ways have been explored to understand why one child differs from another—the problem of individual variation. During the first fifty years of child study in the United States, the two questions were pursued industriously. Extensive studies to follow individuals through the developmental period, such as those conducted at Berkeley, Harvard, and Minnesota, attempted to provide a reliable description of the growing child based on data obtained by following the same children throughout childhood. During the 1920s, J. B. Watson emphasized the significance of early learning in the definition of the child. Sigmund Freud's influence led to greater attention to the critical relation between the early years and the adult personality as he showed the enduring effects of early emotional experiences. Some long-term studies, such as Terman's studies of genius, directed attention to the careers of persons identified early as very bright. By and large, before the second World War child psychologists were most zealous in constructing a photographically accurate portrait of the growing child.

Since the early fifties, psychologists have given new shape to the classical questions about children. New directions were derived in part from the nation's renewed concern with education and with the poor and ill-treated child, and in part from the recognition that a better understanding of the developing child would clarify quite general theoretical issues. Child psychology, like the rest of the discipline, has shown great diversity over the last decade or so, but three organizing ideas have dominated the recent study of development. These ideas are the importance of infancy, the child as constructor of knowledge, and the exceptional child.

The Importance of Infancy

Every major psychological theory places great importance on the nature of the newborn child and on the experiences of the first several years. Concentrated attention on the origin of mind has produced provocative new observations on infant perception and has demonstrated once and for all that the young infant is not a helpless, empty organism. Studies of smiling and early social behavior, related in spirit and procedure to contemporary studies of animal instinct, have begun to clarify the infant's remarkable and rapid transition from a biological to a social organism. Studies of early learning, in the laboratory and in preschools, have demonstrated in the very young child, even in the child of only several hours, a surprising capability to learn. The rather unstructured longitudinal study of the 1930s has been sharpened theoretically and given the support of modern technology in several current investigations of the stability of early individual differences in intelligence and personality.

The complexity of the infant's perception has been nicely illustrated in a study in which pairs of stimuli were presented to children in the first year of life and their choice between them observed (which stimulus will they look toward most often and longest?). Even in the first days of life, human infants show strong preferences among stimuli; movement, complexity, color, and similarity to a human face all seem relevant to the child's interest and attention during the first several months of life. Research in which an infant's eyes are photographed to determine the direction of his gaze has shown that children in the first several days of life are sensitive to contours and to parts of geometric figures displayed in their visual field. By the age of three months the child is not only responding sensitively to different levels of complexity in his environment but is also beginning to anticipate—in a very primitive way, beginning to predict—regular changes in his environment. For example, a three-month-old child who has watched a pattern of moving lights a number of times will begin to shift his eyes to the appropriate place in the visual field even *before* the next light is turned on. Studies such as these help us to understand the perceptual world of the child even before he can speak, and they will permit us to assess more precisely the effects of different kinds of early experience.

A number of child psychologists have taken advantage of electronic and psychophysiological advances to study the stability and development of early differences in personality. One longitudinal study has observed a group of children at four months of age, eight months, thirteen months, twenty-seven months, and will continue to observe them for several years. Videorecords were made of the child's response to his mother, to toys, and to systematically varied visual stimuli. Telemetric procedures have permitted recording heart rate (heart rate deceleration is held by many contemporary observers to be a useful index of attention) even in the freely moving child. Of particular interest are the development of differences in the handling of problems by boys and girls, the apparently stable tendency of some children to be quick and impulsive while others are thoughtful and analytic, and the effects of family structure and parental personality on the development of the child. Observations of this sort still require bringing the child to the laboratory, but there is serious expectation that long-term follow-up studies may be possible in the child's home with telemetric and videorecording procedures unobtrusively registering the natural development and interactions of the young child.

Studies of the sort just described aid in understanding the nature of children's impulses and the best ways to keep them from interfering with orderly social processes and development. The data are relevant to questions about education. Should boys be taught differently from girls? What proportions of school time should be set aside for release of tensions? What mixture of parental responses results in the healthiest outcome for children?

The Child as Constructor of Knowledge

With only a few dissenters, American psychologists between 1913 and 1950 were committed to a conception of the growth in the child as an expanding collection of stimulus-response associations. This conception, which was honored by the philosophical tradition from which American psychology sprang, was buttressed by many analogies from the laboratories of animal learning. The notion of the child as a somewhat passive reflection of environmental contingencies was elegantly simple and productive of many research studies. Several forces have disturbed this simple conception. Of primary consequence, the revival of interest in the discoveries of the Swiss psy-

chologist Jean Piaget and the translation of the larger part of his
work between 1950 and 1960 have set child psychology in the United
States on a new course.

Piaget's view, as shared and modified by other observers, is of a
child beginning with a relatively simple system of reflex adaptations
for dealing with the world he encounters and moving through several
successive stages of cognitive functioning until he achieves adult
notions of time, space, causality, and morality.

The infant begins the first stage as he learns to integrate sensory
information so that, for example, he learns to look at what he
listens to. He also adapts his motor reactions to the information he
gets from the environment. At the beginning of this period an object hidden while the baby watches is no longer existent for him;
by the time the child is two, he has learned to hunt for the hidden
object.

During the period from two to seven years Piaget observed the development of crude symbolic processes; language begins to develop;
games of pretense emerge. But the child still fails to understand certain basic concepts. A child of about four years of age may be able
to recite numbers but has no conception of the one-to-one corre-
spondence of number, names, and objects. Similarly, the young child
is convinced that a ball of clay is changed in quantity when it is
changed in shape. As the child grows older, this conviction is replaced by some cognitive strain or disequilibrium, which paves the
way for the next period.

A finding that has great relevance for educational practice is that
the child between six and ten years will solve problems in an empirical here-and-now fashion, but that children cannot usually solve
problems through abstract symbolic solutions until they are about
twelve years of age. For example, an eight-year-old child can become
quite expert at manipulating the slope of an inclined plane to control
the speed of descent of a toy car but he is almost completely unable
to give any formal abstract statement of the principles involved.
On the other hand, the child of thirteen or fourteen will at once
tackle the problem of the inclined plane in an analytic and deductive
fashion. It has also been demonstrated that there is a regular course
of development in the child's conception of morality and law. This

regularity of development through stages has relevance as well to the building of character and socialization.

The Exceptional Child

Psychologists have long listed as one of their several problems the study of children of exceptionally high and low intelligence, children disturbed in their emotional development, and children who grew up in familial and cultural arrangements different from those of white America. However, pressures within the profession and from the larger community have led to an accelerating expansion of this research.

Earlier studies of young persons who had exceptionally high scores on the Stanford-Binet intelligence test were shown to be better off economically, healthier, taller, and more socially adept than their lower-scoring contemporaries. The general notion that "to them who have shall be given" has serious social consequences when the community attempts to improve the lot of those whose test scores are low. New assessments have been made of the nature of mental retardation with great attention given to an analysis of the motivational and cognitive factors that influence the behavior of the mentally retarded.

Generally, school systems have provided inadequately for the great individual differences among children. The unusually bright child with a rich background of intellectual activities may proceed at his own pace, but often becomes bored, disenchanted and alienated. The child with a modest deficiency in language may be overlooked in the classroom and may fall behind in all areas because of this neglect. Individual instructional techniques, associated with immediate recognition of correct responses, have proved effective in promoting learning even among those persons who score among the lowest on traditional tests of intelligence. Radical therapeutic procedures based on simple learning principles have shown some promise of ameliorating the distress of pathologically fearful and autistic (withdrawn) children.

Child psychologists have engaged in theoretical analysis and have initiated extensive empirical research on early education in urban slums. It is clear that these studies, of great relevance to the community, are inextricably linked to developing theory and research on the nature of infancy and on the child as an active constructor of this thought. The work also has immediate practical usefulness for the young persons involved.

Applications, Present and Future

The three central ideas of developmental psychology have all been directed toward another concept, that of the socialization of the child. Socialization is the process whereby a child adopts the mores of the culture and learns acceptable patterns of social behavior. It has been of interest to psychologists as well as other social scientists. The process is critically important to almost all of the programs of our social institutions.

Two traits clearly related to social development are aggression and dependence. In our culture a well-adjusted person is considered to be self-confident and assertive, but not hostile and exploitively destructive; to be sensitive and considerate, but not passive and exploited. Initially, the socialization process is influenced predominately by parental reactions to the child's behavior. Aggressive or dependent behavior can be encouraged or diminished according to whether the behavior is punished or rewarded. Inconsistent responses on the part of parents often lead to increases in the behavior shown by the child, whether aggressive or dependent.

Psychologists have studied processes of socialization in several ways. Observation of childhood groups has provided much of the information for the development of theories and concepts. Nursery schools have often provided the setting for the observations although special play rooms and specially devised observation rooms are used. For some studies, laboratories in trailers have been used so that investigators might move around to involve various social groups. Some of the experiments have been devised using classic animal behavioral techniques, with principles proposed being tested both with human and animal subjects.

Investigators have observed that in the early years, the child learns to express aggression and dependency partly as a result of imitating those around him. With increased age, he is heavily influenced by peer behavior. In a laboratory situation it has been shown that children will imitate the aggressive behavior of a model but will inhibit the behavior when exposed to films of an aggressive model who has been punished. Characteristic styles of expressing aggressive or dependent behavior emerge by middle adolescence and become resistant to change thereafter, suggesting the important social consequences of exposing children to appropriate models at appropriate stages of development.

Many findings of such studies have great relevance to current issues regarding schooling, early education, and special programs for particular social groups. For example, it has been observed that certain patterns of development occur easily during certain critical periods and afterwards only with great effort; language development is an excellent example. Also, it has been found that sibling position is closely associated with some personality characteristics; the oldest or only child is more likely to be dependent on others and less likely to become a social isolate.

The continuing interest of child psychologists in applying the work of the laboratory to practical issues of society has been seen most recently in applications of behavior therapy and in use of computer-aided instruction in the schools. For example, some desperately autistic children have been brought into sufficient reality contact so that their social isolation can be decreased appreciably by application of principles of response shaping and reinforcement which have been developed in psychological laboratories.

The near future of developmental psychology is clear enough although the speed of technical change makes long-range forecasting chancy. Studies of the first two years of life will continue to grow in number and scope. They will emphasize early language, early social responsiveness, and the growth of concepts of time and space that have been called part of the child's "construction of reality." The study of personality development, again with an emphasis on the years before school, will expand. The longitudinal study is a subtle and effective instrument for answering carefully formulated theoretical problems about the development of personality, and it will continue to be used at least as frequently as it has been in the past. Studies of cognitive and emotional growth around adolescence are beginning to appear.

The evidence of a growing division between generations requires close attention to the changes that take place in children and in the relation between parents and children during the years between ten and twenty.

It is probable, at least in the next decade, that the chief interest of developmental psychologists will be on the child as learner and as problem-solver. In schools and in laboratory arrangements that simulate schools, child psychologists will ask what arrangements of motivational variables, of learning strategies, and of information fed back to the child will provide the best route to generating a community of independent, exploring, and well-informed children with capacity for interaction with others. The proper achievement of these goals—with all their implication for education, including the education of the culturally disadvantaged, the emotionally disturbed, and the retarded child—will require the establishment of additional research centers and demonstration programs that combine the work of developmental psychologists, educators, sociologists, and physicians.

The psychological study of the growing child illustrates the range and variety of phenomena that lie within the domain of psychology. It raises questions of both a biological and a social nature, it explores processes of perception, learning, motivation, thought, and language, and it holds both scientific and practical interest.

7

HOW PEOPLE DIFFER

Psychologists who seek to educe principles of human behavior by laboratory methods generally select each subject on a ran-
dom basis and treat differences between subjects as part of experimental error. Large numbers of psychologists, however, are concerned
with the study of individuals and the way in which human characteristics are associated; therefore, they examine these individual
differences with great interest. Psychologists employed in schools,
industry, hospitals, and clinics or who identify themselves as clinical,
counseling, or industrial psychologists develop and use many devices
aimed at determining when a given person has more or less of a
specific trait, or is above or below average on some measure, or is
more or less likely than the average man to exhibit some particular
form of behavior. Other psychologists classify themselves primarily
as psychometrically oriented or as specialists in the study of personality. They examine statistically and experimentally the ways in
which various personal characteristics are developed in the individual
and the way in which patterns of such characteristics emerge. These
latter investigators do the basic research underlying the extensive
applications of psychological measurement in many parts of our
economy.

Our vocabulary contains many adjectives for describing people.
Vivacious, masculine, withdrawn, hostile, honest, garrulous, persua-

69

sive, stupid, warm, insightful, anxious—these are but a few of the many ways in which people can differ from one another. Psychologists have tried to convert these adjectives from subjective impressions into quantitative measurements. The procedures they devise may take many forms, from a conventional paper-and-pencil test to a week-long trial experience in some carefully planned setting. Sometimes the results have shown that a particular adjective describes some changeable, fluctuating quality of the person. Sometimes the results reveal relatively permanent or stable traits that persist over long periods of time. The stable measures are more useful; they tap something basic about people and enable us to predict how they will behave in the future. Those traits that vary from time to time are also of interest, especially as one tries to understand effects of work and fatigue or monotony, or effects of drugs.

Intelligence Tests

Intelligence tests are the best known of the measures developed by psychologists. Widespread attention to the IQ has had profound effects on the way in which persons in our society think about their children, the likelihood of their success in school and in later life, and about the factors that produce success. Not all of these effects have been beneficial, especially when the importance of a single test score is overrated, and when the nature of the measure is misunderstood.

Since late in the nineteenth century, psychologists have worked to develop appropriate measures to help in sorting out those more likely to succeed in a given activity. The first tests of general ability used the work of laboratory psychologists as a guide, and sought measures of those traits that could be measured reliably. Rapidity of movement, reaction time, the ability to bisect a line accurately, and accuracy in discriminating sounds of different pitch were used in early "intelligence tests" by such investigators as J. McKeen Cattell. Some of the measures he used are given in the following list:

1. Strength of grip, using the dynamometer.
2. Rate of movement: the quickest time in which the hand can be moved through a distance of fifty centimeters.

3. The smallest perceptible distance between two points on the skin, known as "two-point discrimination."

4. Amount of pressure necessary to cause pain by exerting pressure upon the forehead with a strip of hard rubber.

5. The smallest difference in weight which can be discerned, measured by requiring that two weights be lifted in succession.

6. Speed with which an individual can react to a sound.

7. Speed with which an individual can name ten specimens of four different colors arranged in haphazard order.

8. The accuracy with which an individual can bisect a fifty-centimeter line.

9. The accuracy with which an individual can reproduce an interval of ten seconds.

10. Immediate rote memory, using a series of consonants.

Useful test items must possess several characteristics. (1) People must respond differently to them. (2) The same person should score about the same regardless of when he responds to the item. (3) The item response must be related to some important aspect of performance that is to be predicted. The fatal flaw in the list of Cattell items was the lack of relationship between item responses and the performance to be predicted. Speed of response, for example, did not relate to grades earned in courses by the students whom Cattell tested.

Useful measures of intellectual capacity were not found by seeking traits that could be accurately measured but by searching for traits that did relate to other characteristics. Alfred Binet exploited the important fact that intelligence grows with age. He noted that many mental characteristics develop at particular ages and sought to develop test items that would differentiate between age groups. Faced with an immediate need to identify retarded children in French schools, Binet observed items of behavior that were more complex and more nearly representative of the sorts of tasks one learns in school or on a job. His early measures of intelligence were imperfect for several reasons. The items were not well selected, nor were the scoring procedures as accurate as they needed to be; but they did lay the groundwork for improved measurement of intelligence. A sample of the tasks Binet used is presented in the accompanying list:

Age 3

1. Points to nose, eyes, mouth.
2. Repeats sentences of six syllables.
3. Repeats two digits.
4. Enumerates objects in a picture.
5. Gives family name.

Age 8

1. Reads a passage and remembers two items.
2. Adds up the value of five coins.
3. Names four colors: red, yellow, blue, green.
4. Counts backwards from 20 to 0.
5. Writes short sentence from dictation.
6. Gives differences between two objects.

Age 12

1. Repeats seven digits.
2. Gives three rhymes to a word (in one minute).
3. Repeats a sentence of twenty-six syllables.
4. Answers problem questions.
5. Interprets pictures (as contrasted with simple descriptions).

The subsequent work of Lewis Terman in this country led to the development of a much improved test of intelligence, the Stanford Revision of the Binet Scale. For many years Terman's version was considered the standard against which all other measures of intelligence should be compared. Today there are several intelligence tests considerably superior in quality to that early scale.

Both Binet Scale and the Stanford Revision had to be administered individually and required considerable skill on the part of the examiner. The need for an accurate intelligence test that could be given to groups became acute at the beginning of World War I. A number of psychologists joined together to develop the first widely used group test of intelligence, the Army ALPHA Examination. This device was used with considerable success during World War I to both identify recruits unfit for service and to sort out those best qualified for training and advancement.

Schools, industry, and government adapted these early intelligence tests for their own purposes. Psychological testing has become a large industry. Universities and colleges came to use tests as a major part of their processes for selecting each freshman class, and industry began to employ a wide variety of aptitude and ability measures in the selection and classification of employees.

The availability and widespread use of intelligence tests have taught us many things about our society. We have learned, for example, that the policemen, plumbers, electricians, and carpenters are in the main well above average in intelligence; that poor schools depress not only the acquisition of knowledge but also the development of intellectual skills; that our "brightest" young persons come from the "best" homes and from the wealthiest states; that the persons who score lowest on tests of intelligence are also less healthy and more likely to cause social problems. We have also learned that verbal intelligence continues to increase in a person throughout his life span, especially during the periods when he is most active intellectually, and decays only when he begins to deteriorate physically, which it does with the onset of terminal illness.

We would like to use our knowledge of intelligence testing to discover whether the average intelligence is changing; whether, for example, our society with its many cultural features is adding to the average intellectual endowment of our citizens. Little evidence can be educed on this general question, however, since the questions on our intelligence tests have generally sampled the culture in order to see the degree to which each person is affected by it. This means that items in tests devised for such a purpose must be selected with care if they are to be used as constant indicators of absolute intelligence.

Intelligence tests reflect the degree to which an individual has shown himself capable of learning from his culture. Consequently, a person who has lived in an impoverished environment will fail to show, on such a test, how well he might have done if he had lived in a more enriched environment. Many persons' potentialities might be underestimated. This risk is especially great for persons living in isolated areas, persons in families whose native tongue is not English, or whose use of language is minimal, and persons with little school-ing. Tests that are presumably "culture-free" are helpful but provide an inadequate remedy, for they prove to be less useful in predicting success in practical affairs—perhaps because practical performance on the job or in the school also involves a need to know many aspects of the culture.

This alleged dependence of intelligence testing on culture has led many persons to object to most intelligence tests as instruments for preserving the status quo. They point to the use of test scores early in the school life of the child to make decisions about the nature of his educational program that will have long-lasting effects on his future. They point to the low scores obtained by persons from de-prived homes and remind us that the low scores obtained by these persons lead us to provide them with an education inferior to that provided for persons from better homes. They also point out that an individual who has a meager intellectual background is doubly pe-nalized; first, for his lack of background, and second, for the estimate given by the test score indicating that he is not likely to improve in the future because he had not shown evidence of much learning in the past.

It should be noted that the test scores do nothing more than record in one more way the association between impoverished en-vironment and socially undesirable traits of the persons who reside in them. The test scores themselves do not provide any evidence about causal relations and cannot be used by themselves as direct evidence of innate deficiencies in the residents of such areas. They do, nonetheless, lead us to believe that the deficits in potentialities of such residents are likely to persist throughout their lives, since for all other subgroups in our society we have observed that intel-ligence test scores change little with age.

Without doubt, there are many abuses of intelligence and aptitude tests. Also without doubt, many tests place too much reliance on items that are influenced by factors closely associated with socio-economic status. Nonetheless, test scores of this sort can also serve to aid persons from deprived backgrounds. If appropriate tests were developed for such groups and the score of an individual person were interpreted in terms of his own background, it would be pos-sible to identify those persons who can profit from additional investment in their education. Just as we do not assume that every person from a privileged home can attain membership in Phi Beta Kappa, so we should not assume that every person from a disadvantaged home does not merit advanced education or must become unemployable. Within each social group there are substantial individual differences in potentiality. To identify those for whom an investment is likely to be most profitable benefits both our society and the individuals concerned.

This point pertains to one basic and appropriate objection to the use of psychological tests for employment or admission to educational programs. No test is sufficiently accurate to predict with precision what each individual would achieve. The tests have value because there is *some* relationship. A group of persons who score high on an appropriate test will include a larger proportion of high achievers than would a group of persons making low scores. Yet even in the latter group, some individuals might do very well. The problem is one of sorting them out.

Psychologists have become increasingly dissatisfied with the use of a single score for such predictions. Analysis of the nature of intelligence suggests that it has many components. In addition, basic studies of factors leading to success, or to choice of persons as leaders, and of persons who have been proven to be creative have shown the great diversity in combinations of characteristics that may lead to eminence or to outstanding work. Good practice in psychological testing today involves the use of not one test but a battery of tests, so that one may sample more than one aspect of ability and include measures of motivation, interests, and personality characteristics.

Personality Tests

Anyone who attends carefully to human characteristics is quickly impressed by the wide variety of characteristics that can affect the ability of an individual to use his capabilities. The early success in the measurement of intelligence led many investigators to seek similar devices to measure other characteristics which were not essentially intellectual. The earliest successful devices of this sort were the personality tests, first developed in group form for use during World War I, then later expanded into the more complex instruments used during World War II and subsequently by government, industry, schools, and hospitals.

A typical personality test includes a large number of items asking how an individual feels, thinks, or responds. Sample items from personality inventories might include those in the following list:

I sometimes think nobody likes me.
I daydream a great deal.
I have frequent spells of nausea, dizziness, and vomiting.
Sometimes I feel as though I have a tight band around my head.
I like almost every person I meet.
I would be willing to sneak into a theatre if I thought I would not be caught.
I like to drive very fast.
I always have a good reason for doing whatever I do.

Personality inventories can be scored in various ways. One frequent procedure is to administer a large number of items of this sort to people already known to possess some particular characteristic, for example, hospital samples of persons diagnosed as having paranoid tendencies, or as schizophrenics, or as having anxiety disorders may be used. Items that are characteristic of each of these groups can then comprise the scoring key for a given dimension. Some personality scales yield scores on psychopathic deviation, schizophrenia, paranoia or the like. Other inventories use groups more nearly in the normal range as their criteria for the development of scoring keys; they yield scores which describe such aspects of personality as introversion, anxiety, depression, and so forth. Still other inventories are scored in terms of the patterns of responses that are typical of persons in the general population. Certain items tend to be responded to in the same way, and so yield clusters which are assumed to reflect some stable, consistent characteristic of individuals. The scores from such inventories can then be studied to determine the patterning of such traits in the general population.

Studies of personality tests that are scored in this complex fashion have led to a heightened interest in the examination of the multiple measures that can be obtained for individual subjects. A major effort in psychology is directed toward this multivariate analysis of the characteristics of individuals. The goal is to eliminate the great variety of adjectives that can describe different individuals and instead to describe them using the major dimensions of human personality: Because these dimensions are not too numerous, orderly groupings of individuals of similar characteristics are possible.

The availability of high-speed computers with huge memories makes possible this sort of analysis of human characteristics on a large scale. Variables for study can include not merely measures of intelligence and special aptitudes and measures of personality, but also measures of the values held by individuals, their preferences for occupations of one sort or another, factors relating to the attitudes about them held by their peers and superiors, and measures of their performance in important assignments of one sort or another. The use of multivariate analysis in these areas has likely payoff for improved selection of employees, improved counseling of individuals in occupational choice, and in improved understanding of factors that influence major movements in modern societies.

Individual Differences in Business and Industry

Psychologists have played an increasingly important role in the improved utilization of personnel in government, business, and industry. Adequate attention to individuals, their differences, and their potentialities has been a critical factor in the development of management potential, in the development of improved worker attitudes, and in increasing productivity.

Most of the psychologists working in this field are involved in three major kinds of functions: (1) personnel selection, training and job analysis, and analysis of production processes; (2) development and evaluation of managerial personnel; and (3) analysis of complex systems and development of techniques for the management of production or information. In many of these operations, psychologists join with sociologists, occasionally political analysts, computer scientists, and applied mathematicians.

The first function, namely, personnel training, job analysis, job design, and the melding of human capabilities with the machine specifications is, in a sense, the best-known, tried-and-true, well-developed area of applied psychology. Job analysis and job design date back to pre-World War I practitioners of industrial production improvement. The measurement of aptitudes and abilities began prior to World War I. The application of psychological test techniques to the selection of pilots, bombardiers, and navigators in World War II is indeed one of the success stories of applied psychology and illustrates the usefulness of psychological work. The formidable prospect of selecting huge numbers of untried young men for training as military fliers encouraged the Army Air Corps to enlist the services of psychologists. These, in turn, perfected a battery of simple tests which were employed in testing about one thousand applicants for pilot training in the early 1940s. The parties who were responsible at that time for training permitted *all* of the tested pilots to enter training; that is, their psychological scores did not affect the decision as to who would and would not be given training. The value of the tests in selecting apt young men for pilot training and in singling out those who had low or little aptitude was quickly (and impressively) shown by this trial, and the tests were used throughout the war in selecting pilot, bombardier, and navigator trainees. The tests saved not only many lives but hundreds of thousands of dollars in effort wasted in training those who were unsuited for flying jobs.

Psychologists are involved in work on a variety of human engineering problems, including the design of equipment, the selection of personnel to operate it, and the development of training schemes as well as training devices. Psychologists have been engaged in the design of the cockpits and control systems of all major aircraft since the P-51, in the radar systems and associated equipment of their control, in design of the capsules in which men have been launched into space and the communication and control systems connected with these craft.

Most of the new jobs associated with technical advances in the aerospace industries have produced enormous problems in training appropriate personnel. Here again psychologists have played an important role. First in the analysis of the job to be done; then in the selection of people with ability to do it; third in the design of training routines and special devices, including simulators and trainers to perfect the learners' skill in operating complex equipment.

Another area of training and training development depending strongly on the ability of psychologists has been management training, especially that related to improving executives' performance and increasing their skill in problem solving and group management or leadership. As enterprises have grown more complex and the demands on their managers more sophisticated, the need has arisen for training of managerial incumbents and candidates in skills of rational problem solving, and in techniques and methods of enhancing group morale, work performance, motivation, responsibility, and cooperation. The educational programs have also included attention to personality problems, to effects of emotional involvements, and to delicate matters of interpersonal relationships. It is common practice for managers to enroll in specialized courses lasting fom a few days to a couple of months. The courses are conducted by psychologists and the training materials employed are generally designed by psychologists. The important feature of the training is that it is based upon sound psychological analysis of job requirements and job performance and that the methods for presenting material and teaching it are also grounded in scientific principles.

Involvement of psychologists in problems of management training has paralleled their increasing concern with the development of methods for improving the efficiency of complex systems. The psychologist has worked, for example, with medical systems, law enforcement and the rehabilitation of prisoners, waste management, and even the economic development of entire nations. In contrast to the subsidiary role that he has generally played in the design of mechanical equipment and training devices where the specifications for the job have been dictated by engineering or physical science requirements, the psychologist has been concerned with "front-end analysis" in the development of so-called "civil systems" work. This means that the specifications for the design or revision of the system in question are not dictated by considerations lying outside the behavioral sciences but rather are arrived at through analysis of the problem in terms of social and behavioral factors per se. To a very large extent the important variables involved in such systems are variables of human capacity, attitude, predisposition, intention, and tendency to particular kinds of behavior. Thus in health, education, and transportation systems, while there are technical constraints, the most important factors very often are human disposition to use or not use technology that is available. In a most striking and crucial sense, this is also true for emergency planning where psychologists have been heavily involved in assisting city, state, and other authorities in developing plans for handling emergencies such as floods and fires, riots, civil disorders, and war. To a great extent, this activity has consisted in developing techniques for training those responsible for operating emergency systems to cope quickly with these emergencies and to use information resources fully.

Individual Differences and Education

National concern for the improvement of education at all levels has grown rapidly in the past several years. Most Americans have accepted the idea that schooling is good for everyone, that schools provide an avenue to social betterment, that education provides useful practical ways of achieving success in a competitive society, that schools provide a major social institution through which racial discrimination can be eliminated, and that education constitutes a sifting process through which the better minds are selected for complex tasks in society—in short, that education within our school system provides the primary basis for improvement of our society.

Can we really take into account individual differences across children and develop educational programs that truly realize the potentialities of each individual? Seeking the means for accomplishing genuine individualized instruction on a large-scale basis is a most important national goal although it is exceedingly difficult to achieve. It is impossible at present to show more than superficial recognition of individual differences in the typical classroom. The same instructional sequence is given every child in a self-contained classroom with a single teacher. This is where new educational technology is desperately needed and where some real promise of providing major answers to the question of quality education for everyone may lie.

The individualizing of instruction at all ages from preschool through adult education is a major objective of most research and development work in education today. Emphasis is upon the learner rather than the teacher. The student begins at that point in the curriculum where he is most capable of learning and moves at his own rate with his performance being immediately rewarded or disapproved. To keep track of each person moving at his own pace in a continuous progress environment where the particular branching of the curriculum is tailor-made for his own learning aptitudes and level, requires a computer to manage the curriculum and assist with the instruction. The rapid growth of computers in education, the development of programmed instruction, and the entry of a number of major companies in the computer field joining together with textbook publishers and research and development centers has resulted in the emergence of a new interdisciplinary field generally known as computer-assisted instruction.

Individualized instruction demands a fusion of learning technology, repeated diagnostic testing, and close integration of large data files for problem solving, career planning, and self-examination by the student. And in turn, the budding technology clearly needs more powerful theoretical formulations and scientific research of a basic nature if it is to avoid sterility and mismanagement.

Psychologists are heavily involved in all aspects of computer-assisted instruction as well as other forms of individualized instruction. A greatly increased amount of fundamental work must be undertaken in learning and motivation, in perception and cognition, and in the measurment of human abilities, all within the challenging new context of individualized instruction made possible by the computer in education. It is already apparent that the present prototype systems are only the primitive forerunners of what is to come.

In its enthusiasm to embark upon large-scale developmental programs in education, the federal government has given low priority to individual project research and the nurturance of high quality basic research, with the result that promising young research workers and many seasoned behavioral scientists are being diverted in large numbers to administrative, development, and demonstrational activities, a trend which may actually impede some aspects of scientific progress in education. It is important that this imbalance be corrected as soon as possible.

It is evident that psychology, more than any other academic discipline, has a crucial role to play in meeting these new challenges while at the same time taking advantage of the unparalleled opportunities for scientific development in those fields of psychology which can best be studied in an educational context.

From all of these studies both of abilities and of personality characteristics, a number of important generalizations come forward. For one thing, an individual who scores in the socially desired direction on all characteristics is very rare indeed. Likewise, the person who makes no such scores is very rare. Within each individual, regardless of the overall average level of his scores, one can generally find many areas in which he has highly useful characteristics and many areas in which he does not.

Just as there are wide differences in an individual's characteristics as we move from trait to trait, so there are wide differences in a given trait as we move from group to group. On measure of aggression, for example, policemen scored much higher than artists. On scores of verbal and quantitative intelligence, physicists score higher than painters, who in turn score higher than bench operators in a factory. On measures of economic motivation, salesmen score higher than school teachers. Yet within all group comparisons, one can find many persons within each group who score higher than some persons in the other group. In general, one finds much greater variation within each of these groups than between group averages. This diversity should give pause to those who want to make general statements about particular groups.

The widespread use of psychological tests has led to a considerable outcry about the use of the scores and about the nature of the items included in the tests themselves. Many persons would argue that a detailed examination of the characteristics of an individual is not to that person's self interest. Others would argue that it is improper to subject an individual to that sort of scrutiny, even if he makes himself a willing subject. The argument is made that measuring the characteristics of human beings constitutes an invasion of privacy or somehow reduces the rights of the individual.

Good practice in psychology requires that testing be done with the informed consent of the person tested and that scores obtained in such testing be used in the precise manner indicated at the time consent for testing was given. The American Psychological Association has made explicit requirements in this area a part of its published

Code of Ethics, and has, in addition, prepared a manual on technical requirements for tests and related psychological measures.

The concern about potential invasions of privacy is not wholly unwarranted. Psychological measures of the sort we have described can serve the prejudiced, the curious, and the man of ill will just as well as they can serve the individual who desires to improve the lot of man and the quality of human life. Recent studies of the propriety of certain practices in psychological investigations have revealed instances in which improper procedures were employed. These discoveries have led the professional societies and the graduate departments of psychology to institute programs to upgrade ethical practices and introduce knowledge about proper procedures that should be employed in investigations of human characteristics. The psychologist has played a critical role in attainments of our society thus far, and can contribute a great deal more. Improvements in measures of intelligence, personality characteristics, and of values, interests, and preferences have depended on continuing basic work in psychometrics, in multivariate analysis, and in studies of substantial segments of the population. Adequate safeguards exist to assure that this fundamental work is carried on responsibly. It deserves continuing and increasing support.

8
PERSONS

A major portion of the field of psychology relates directly to the promotion of well-being and adequate functioning of individuals. This is evidenced not merely by the large numbers of persons employed in hospitals and clinics, or in private practice, but also by the emphasis in research programs, training activities, and in programs of diagnosis and prevention in schools and communities. Approximately two-thirds of all psychologists report that their greatest scientific competence is related to the problems of individuals and their mental health. The most direct involvement is by clinical psychologists, school psychologists, or those in counseling and guidance. They comprise more than half of the population of American psychologists. Their work includes four primary areas of concern: direct service to patients and clients, teaching, administration, and research. About half of these psychologists are employed by educational institutions (including colleges and universities, secondary schools, and medical schools). An additional 35 percent are employed by governmental bodies and nonprofit organizations (chiefly hospitals and clinics).

Research confirms the common sense recognition that personality disorders often begin early in life and become increasingly difficult to alter. The need, therefore, to devote considerable research effort to further our understanding of psychopathology of childhood and for the development of programs of prevention utilizing early intervention is apparent. Nowhere is this more apparent than in the diagnosis, treatment, and prevention of mental retardation.

The utilization of psychologists in the mental health field is by no means restricted to clinic and hospitalized patients. Persons throughout the spectrum of adjustment have occasion for counseling services, most notably young people with less severe problems of personal adjustment and those in need of vocational and educational guidance. Probably all students—and certainly those who have been unable to make a satisfactory work adjustment or to obtain optimal educational or training experiences—can profit from such psychological assistance.

Great advances have been made in recent years in providing aid to those members of society who require counseling on problems of employment, or education, or occupational choice, or in family relations, marital discord, or social relations. The programs of the Office of Education, of the Vocational Rehabilitation Administration, and of the Veteran's Administration have increased the number and the competence of counselors who aid individuals with problems of this sort. Industry has increased its own capabilities as a result of growing awareness of the loss of human potential that can otherwise occur.

Entry into a life of useful employment requires a person to use our educational system in its most effective way in terms of his characteristics and goals. No segment of the society needs more help in making proper choices than our disadvantaged youth, especially the young black male. Even with the major programs in psychology that have been developed with massive federal help, there are few persons available to move into this important area of work and do a competent job. The number of well-trained counseling psychologists is far too small for this task alone and thus not nearly large enough for all of the other areas of work where their efforts could increase the well-being and the productivity of our citizens. This is especially regrettable when it is so clear that there are large numbers of capable young persons highly motivated to work on precisely these problems.

In spite of an impression that may have been given in the preceding chapters psychologists know that a person is not just a collection of physiological and psychological processes. Valuable

as the analytic method is in science, it does not cause us to lose
sight of the integrity of the whole individual. Psychologists whose
work entails helping people have this fact thrust upon them
repeatedly, and perhaps the best way to illustrate it is to cite
case histories.

EMOTIONALLY DISTURBED CHILDREN

The eight-year-old child appeared very tense and ap-
prehensive when the psychologist asked her to leave her mother
and accompany him to a playroom he used for psychological examinations. The mother had visited him the day before to discuss the
difficulty she was having in persuading her daughter to go to school.
For some time the child had become quite anxious each morning
before school, couldn't eat her breakfast, and complained of pain
and nausea. Her mother had taken her to the pediatrician on three
occasions in the past month. The doctor could find no physical basis
for the child's symptoms and he suggested that the mother talk
with the teacher to determine whether there had been some incident
at school that might be bothering the girl. The teacher could
think of nothing that might be a basis for the fearful reaction,
but did report that the child was rather shy, was particularly
nervous when asked to read aloud, had become more withdrawn
recently, but that each day she did come to school she appeared
increasingly comfortable as the day progressed. After the third
trip to the pediatrician he suggested that the parents seek psychological consultation. The mother told the psychologist that her
daughter appeared quite ill most mornings, was tearful, and had
stomachaches and headaches. The mother said that she found it
very difficult to force a sick child to go to school though that had
been the advice of both the pediatrician and the teacher. She did
note that when she permitted the girl to remain at home, because
she was sick, she felt better rapidly and spent the rest of the day
following her mother about the house, ostensibly helping with the
housekeeping tasks. It was obvious to the mother that the child con-
stantly was seeking her attention. How could the psychologist help?

A thorough understanding of why a person acts as he does requires that we know considerably more about him than what would be covered generally in a personality characterization. The total person is also a function of his biological makeup, his social condition, his interests, his aptitudes, his abilities, the values and the knowledge he has acquired from his training and experiences, and the opportunities for growth available to him. How a person will behave in any given situation will depend on these multiple and interacting factors.

The psychologist conducted a thorough examination of all of these factors. He used three primary methods in this evaluation: these were data from informants (the parents, the teacher, the physician); his own direct observations of the child in interviews; data from psychological tests.

Data from Informants

Evidence from the pediatrician's repeated examinations convincingly indicated that the girl's physical condition could not account for the pain and anxiety she was suffering. The psychologist found from the teacher and from his interviews with the mother and with the child herself that the girl came from a generally secure and happy home but that she had few friends and preferred to remain indoors playing alone or helping her mother. Her mother said that she and her husband rarely went out in the evenings because it was so upsetting to their daughter to have a baby-sitter. She also noted that her daughter's symptoms did not occur on Saturdays, were present but manageable on Sundays when the whole family went to church, and were more severe on Mondays than other weekdays. The girl was interested in learning how to cook and sew and her favorite game was to play house.

The psychologist found from his talks with the mother that the family had lost their only other child in infancy two years before their daughter was born. The parents had married late in life and could not have more children. Since the birth of their daughter the mother acknowledged that she had been unduly protective of her.

Intellectual Capacity and Achievement

The psychologist gave the girl some tests to assess her intelligence, the level of her skills in school achievement, and her personality. Compared with other children of her age, the girl's intelligence capacity was average. The teacher had said that she worked hard in school and obtained average grades. The parents helped the girl in reading at home and said they hoped she would want to go to college. The girl told the psychologist that she considered herself to be a very poor student, she believed that she was retarded.

The methods for measuring achievement are much the same as those used in assessing intelligence. That is, items are selected which differentiate among persons with varying amounts of education. Scores are usually given in terms of grade equivalents, thus a score of 3.5 in arithmetic would indicate that a child's ability in arithmetic is halfway through the third grade. In this case the psychologist found the girl to be just slightly behind the average of her third grade class in reading and about on par with them in the other basic skills of arithmetic and spelling.

Personality

Research with personality inventories has shown that despite the fact that each of us is unique, personality traits can be ordered into some twenty or fewer dimensions that can account for most characteristics judged to be important in interpersonal relations (cf. Chapter 7). The pattern of scores a given person obtains on a personality test can be compared with patterns of other groups to give an indication of the degree to which a person is similar or different in personality from individuals having psychiatric disorders, for example, or criminal tendency, or who are judged to be mentally healthy.

Another avenue to the assessment of personality is through an understanding of the inner mental life of an individual, that is to say, by studying his fantasies, his perceptual patterns, his cognitive style, and the content of his imagery. A subject is given the opportunity to impose a pattern upon an inherently unstructured stimulus, such as an ink blot, or to invent a coherent story about a relatively ambiguous picture. In doing so the person reveals the principles he used, and thereby reflects both his neurophysiological makeup and the experiences he has had in living. He is said to project his own style of organizing events, to relate his own way of perceiving interpersonal relationships. Persons with known forms of psychopathology tend to give responses that are characteristic of the disorder from which they suffer.

In this case the child's invented story suggested that she was a shy little girl who believed that she was a disappointment to her parents and feared the loss of their affection. Further interviewing and observations of the girl in the playroom showed that she needed frequent reassurances of her mother's love and safety which she could insure by constant contact with her mother. Furthermore she feared embarrassment at school because she had missed so much and the others were moving farther ahead of her.

Treatment

In talking with the teacher, the psychologist found that the teacher had had the girl work especially hard on those days she was in school because the teacher was trying to help her catch up. The teacher agreed to reduce the amount of oral recitation required until the girl had learned the material already completed by the rest of the class, and to spend extra time in tutoring in order to speed the process. The mother was enabled to see that it was important to get the child back into school immediately. Psychological studies have shown, as common sense suggests, that if a child's fear and physical discomfort are relieved by staying away from school, then the child will learn to avoid that situation.

But both the child and the teacher reported that her symptoms improved considerably once she was in school. And so the mother was encouraged to awaken the child later in the morning and get her to school quickly, rather than prolonging her stay at home. With further consultation with the teacher and further work with the child and her mother, the child's social skills improved, she did well in her school work, and the mother's apprehensions diminished.

MARRIAGE COUNSELING

Perhaps the most frequent manifestation of psychological difficulty is seen in the most intimate of all relationships, marriage. Many people believe that sexual incompatibility is the major cause of troubled marriages. Although sex is often a factor, conflict over money is far more common, and conflict regarding roles of dominance, or dependence, of child rearing practices, and trouble with in-laws are frequently core issues. Psychologists who practice marriage counseling find that the husbands and wives who consult them do not communicate. They may express great affection for each other (as well as great anger), they may talk a great deal, but neither really understands what the other is thinking and feeling or how to meet the needs of the other because his or her own needs do not seem to be met.

The psychologist in the role of marriage counselor is neither a judge nor a referee. If he is successful, the partners will see their behavior as others do rather than as each had thought his own was projected; each will no longer reinterpret the behavior of the spouse, but will understand the message as it was meant rather than as his expectations and anger led him to hear it.

For example, a wife with children in school wished to take a part-time job doing clerical work in a downtown office (she had done office work before her marriage). Her husband absolutely forbade her to do so; he said a wife and mother belong at home. He pointed out that he certainly expected to support the family as he always had. Besides, he said, the house was a mess and she should spend more time cleaning up at home instead of daydreaming about an exciting life downtown or drinking coffee with her friends in the neighborhood. The wife said she didn't know how her husband would know whether she were home or not, or if the house were clean or not, because he never stayed home. He called nearly every evening saying he must work late, slept all morning Saturday, listened to a game in the afternoon, and played golf all day Sunday. She complained that he wouldn't listen to problems she was having with the children or help maintain the house. He replied that she had let herself go, so who would want to come home? He was concerned about the children, but he felt they were getting along all right; their mother worried too much. And he asked if a man who works extra hours all week shouldn't have a few hours of rest and recreation during his time off.

This sort of downward spiral leads to acrimony, bitterness, emotional damage to the children as well as to the adults involved, and eventually to divorce. As the psychological distance between these people becomes greater, their ability to communicate deteriorates, they distort their interpretation of the other's behavior and become defensive about their own. What was each of these persons trying to tell the other? Certainly neither was being supportive of the other. There was insufficient mutuality of interest and concern. Each felt rejected by the other. After a series of interviews with the psychologist, the husband gradually came to accept the view that his wife's interest in work was not intended as an insult to his competence to support the family, but an effort to express her own inner needs. The wife gained sufficient insight to understand that her husband's absence and apparent indifference were not so much a rejection of her as a search for sympathetic concern about his professional advancement, which he found early in the marriage but lost when the children were young. As each began to show a renewed concern for the needs of the other, their own needs became increasingly satisfied.

AGING

Nearly every family faces or will face the problem of a long period of living after retirement. Those without plans, without interests outside of their work (men about their jobs; women wrapped up in the care of their children) are likely to suffer most and to bring suffering to their families.

For example, a lady in good health in her early sixties came to see a psychologist about her husband, a man nearing seventy who had retired four years earlier. He had been a fire marshal for forty years and gained much respect for the work he had done with others in reducing the incidence and damage from fire. After retirement he had little to do, whereas his wife had a routine of housekeeping, shopping, and visiting that she tried to maintain. She complained that he followed her around the house for hours, that he used poor judgment when he accompanied her on shopping trips (their income was now more limited), that he sulked when her friends visited, and that their friends increasingly avoided visiting as his condition worsened. He was not eating well; and he slept poorly, disrupting her routine with his insomnia and early rising. She had found it necessary to nag him about his personal appearance. Lately he did not seem to talk sense some of the time. She feared she was making matters worse. Sometimes she felt sympathy, but frequently she was irritated. She didn't know what to do. She wondered if he were becoming senile. When the psychologist saw the husband it was clear that he was profoundly depressed; his life had lost much of its meaning.

Brain pathology is not uncommon in older persons. Deteriorative diseases easily affect the delicate tissues of the nervous system. Among the most common are diseases of the heart and circulatory system which reduce the metabolic efficiency of the body and may cause damage to the brain. Perhaps the most serious are cerebral vascular accidents or strokes, sometimes slight or undetected. A more insidious degeneration may occur with increased age as a less efficient circulatory system provides increasingly less adequate support for the nervous system. Lack of adequate sensory stimulation and reduction in movement can also cause disruption in perceptual processes and in thinking.

In this case, therefore, the psychologist was particularly interested in assessing the possible biological basis for the man's symptoms. A period of hospitalization was recommended. In the hospital the patient was carefully examined by the neurologist and an internist, as well as by a psychiatrist and the psychologist. He was found to be in generally good health, though there was some reduction in his reactions generally. He spoke and moved and responded slowly. However no pathology could be found in his nervous, circulatory, or other organ systems.

Psychological research has shown that a number of behavioral tests of thinking, of perception, of memory, and of motor skills can detect various kinds of brain pathology. The psychologist examined the patient using these techniques and found the man could function well in all of them except for general retardation in timing and movements noted by everyone who observed him. The personality tests confirmed the psychiatric diagnosis that the patient's loss of purpose had resulted in severe depression of mood, the several concomitants of which include retardation of movement, disturbed sleeping and eating patterns, and neglect of personal hygiene and appearance. In the hospital he was given medication to help relieve his symptoms and was provided with a routine of activities. The psychologist noticed that he seemed to move with more spirit and interest when asked to help out with ward activities, especially when it involved assisting other patients. The psychologist and the social worker evolved a discharge plan for the patient as he improved which utilized his interest in helping others. The patient joined a service club whose special project was volunteer work in a local hospital. He became more and more active in the organization, until it occupied a significant portion of his time. His home life was greatly improved, many patients benefited from his helpful interest in them, many other volunteers were given renewed meaning in their own lives as he recruited them, and he lived a cheerful, constructive "retirement."

THE INDIVIDUAL HOSPITALIZED IN A MENTAL HOSPITAL

On a state hospital ward, there is a nurse smiling as she hands a small plastic token to a clean shaven, neatly dressed, gray haired, elderly man. She tells him that he received the token because of his neat appearance. He thanks her and is obviously pleased with himself. He has earned this token just as he has earned other tokens during the day by his own efforts for working in a productive job, self-grooming, and care of his quarters. He will spend his tokens for the many available "good" things in the hospital such as a chance to see a movie, to play Ping-Pong, or a pass to go off the ward. Only a few weeks ago this patient, having been hospitalized for twenty years, sat in a chair all day, apathetic, withdrawn, soiled, unshaven, and disheveled, a zombie dead to the world.

One of the recent exciting developments in the field of rehabilitation of hospitalized psychiatric patients has been the introduction by psychologists of behavior modification procedures such as the "token economy" program described above. These programs, in large part, derive from the earlier laboratory reinforcement studies introduced by Skinner and other experimental psychologists (described in Chapter 3 of this report in the section on reinforcement). The techniques used illustrate the generalization from research on animals, research that was originally far removed from any apparent practical application. The laboratory principles grew out of repeated demonstrations in the animal laboratory that behavior is governed by its rewarding or punishing consequences. Observations of hospital routine had pointed up that undesirable behaviors of mental patients such as apathy, withdrawal, and even hallucinations were often reinforced and unintentionally supported by the hospital staff. The new hospital procedures which have been developed require the therapist to make clear decisions as to what specific behaviors would be most helpful for each individual patient. Also, an appropriate reward must be presented immediately upon the appearance of such behaviors in order to reinforce them.

Perhaps the most important element of change introduced into the hospital situation as a result of these newer techniques is the training of the aides, nurses, and other hospital personnel in the proper response to individual patients. It is the staff of the hospital who can and do control the reinforcing consequences for patients with food, cigarettes, and human contact. Thus the basic principles of learning developed years earlier in a psychology laboratory now permit radical changes in the treatment of patients in mental hospitals. An important side effect is the attitude of the staff which becomes more optimistic concerning the possibility of change, as the staff sees that even people hospitalized for many years can and do behave differently. The staff then displays a greater respect toward the patient as an individual human being who can eventually leave the hospital.

Developments such as the token economy have particularly influenced the treatment of the long-term institutionalized patients. With such developments has come the recognition that one of the great influences on the incoming patient in a mental hospital is the effects of institutionalization itself. Thus the emphasis has switched to getting the newly admitted patient out of the hospital as quickly as possible, preferably within six months to a year at the most. More people are now entering the mental hospitals but even more are being discharged; hence there is a decline in total hospital population.

Related developments have accentuated optimism about the improvability of the mental hospital patient's behavior as a consequence of intensive research efforts by psychologists in recent years. These developments have included day hospitals, night hospitals, sheltered workshops, therapeutic communities, newer tranquilizing and energizing drugs, recognition of the legal rights of hospitalized patients, and the movement of research and professional teams directly into the community including the home. Generally, all these developments have broken down the sharp distinction between the hospital and the community, have helped the patient bridge the gap back to the community, have helped end the apathetic and custodial atmosphere of the old style mental hospital, have enhanced the importance and stature, if not the salary, of the hospital employee, and have enhanced the likelihood that people who need help will seek it and get it in the mental hospital.

In these developments the psychologist has been a researcher, clinician, administrator, interdisciplinary worker, and, perhaps most important of all, an inspirer of the belief in change—change in patients, change in staff, and change in institutions. The past decade has shown that there is a clear relationship between the amount of money a state or federal agency is willing or able to spend on personnel and research and the chances of the hospitalized mental patient being helped with his problems and returned to the community as a productive member. The psychological problems of people— even normal people leading ordinary lives—are influenced by multiple forces too complex to be properly appreciated from any single provincial point of view. They cannot be reduced to laboratory experiments or overlooked in social statistics. They must be dealt with as intelligently as possible in the light of whatever information and experience the clinical psychologist can muster. The improvement of such services must be regarded as one of the most important goals of psychological science. The preparation of adequate numbers of professionally qualified persons must be given high priority by our universities.

The data presented later in this report suggest a growth rate which will provide about 2,000 doctoral degrees per year in psychology by 1971. Other data indicate that as many as two-thirds of these will have a primary interest in some aspects of psychology related to the mental health field. Even so, clearly, psychology's contribution to the manpower needs in the mental health field over the next several years will fall substantially below the nation's needs. To help close the gap it will be necessary to provide two kinds of effort: greatly expanded programs of training for mental health workers, including psychologists; and greatly expanded programs of research, both basic and clinical. We would, therefore, urge that continued federal assistance and increased local support be provided for training psychologists and for construction and staffing of mental health and mental retardation facilities.

Of all of the professions with a primary involvement in the field of mental health, psychology is the only one which provides extensive graduate education in research design and methodology. An important function of psychologists working in government agencies, hospitals, clinics, college counseling centers, and medical schools is their involvement in research and program evaluation. Improved methods of identification, prevention, and treatment, and implementation of programs having built-in feedback of efficacy are the result of their work. Such research results in more efficient use of personnel, as shown, for example, in the application of principles of learning to the modification of psychotic behavior described earlier in this chapter.

9

THE SOCIAL NATURE
OF MAN

The fact that men are shaped by their contacts with other men has been implied or discussed in most of the preceding chapters. Indeed, men's ability to exert profound influence over one another's behavior has been a source of interest not only to psychologists but also to sociologists, political and economic scientists, and cultural anthropologists. It is within this wide spectrum of interests that social psychology has fashioned its province—a concern with understanding the social nature of the individual, understanding how his thoughts, feelings, and behavior are influenced by the actual or implied presence of others.

The major work of many social psychologists is in the laboratory. As objects of study they may use a small group of persons working on an assigned task, or individuals engaged in a game or contest, or a larger group of persons to assess the effects of a given method of persuasion. Their laboratories require facilities and equipment for observation and recording, equipment for presentation of stimulus materials, and sometimes quite elaborate apparatus to simulate real life conditions.

Other social psychologists may work essentially as test developers and analyzers, or may conduct surveys of opinions and attitudes, or may engage in mathematical analyses aimed at obtaining more useful representations of the structure of values and beliefs in a society. Still other social psychologists may work in the classroom, in a com-

97

munity agency, or in business or government, and become concerned with the education of persons whose duties require greater sensitivity to the views of others, or may suggest management procedures to improve working relationships and communications. The problems studied may vary; however, all of them have direct and immediate relevance to the many problems facing our society today.

Attitudes

One of the ways in which social psychologists have attempted to understand the interrelatedness of thoughts, feelings, and behavior has been by studying the circumstances which lead to the formation and change of attitudes. Most psychologists regard an attitude as a disposition, acquired through previous experience, to react to certain things, people, or events in positive or negative ways. Attitudes represent a tendency to approach or avoid that which maintains or threatens the things one values. Like the values from which they are often derived, attitudes have an effect upon and are consistently related to beliefs and behavior.

Although we recognize in a general way that our attitudes influence us in various ways, few people are aware of the pervasiveness of this phenomenon. Psychologists have detected the influence of attitudes in the kind of information people acquire, the facts they remember, the motives they attribute to others, their ability to reason, their predictions about the effectiveness of remedial programs, the way they classify information, and even what they see. The unconscious influence of negative attitudes toward a social group on judgments about the effectiveness of social policies related to that group represents an instance of this phenomenon with important practical implications. This influence is so consistent that a decision maker seeking advice in which judgment plays a major role should undoubtedly listen both to supporters and opponents of the social group involved.

A good deal of research has indicated that attitudes and beliefs tend to be consistently related. A doctor, for example, who has a negative attitude toward Medicare may believe that Medicare will interfere with high medical standards. On the other hand, a doctor with a positive attitude toward Medicare will probably have no such belief. In fact, such a doctor may even believe that Medicare will produce high medical standards. This consistency between attitude and belief provides the basis for one approach to changing attitudes. If the beliefs that support an attitude are changed, the attitude itself will tend to change. If, for example, the doctor with a negative attitude toward Medicare could be convinced that Medicare would not interfere with high medical standards, professional freedom, and other such values, there would be a tendency for him to alter his negative stance toward Medicare.

In our highly interdependent society efforts to change attitudes abound. Some of these efforts, like those of advertisers and of political and religious leaders, are organized and explicit. Others like those of parents, friends, and acquaintances are entirely informal.

Psychologists studying attitude change approach the matter from several directions. One group looks at the political speech, the clergyman's sermon, the teacher's lecture, and the advertiser's message and abstracts from these superficially different activities the concept of persuasive communication. Taking this as his research focus he studies the influence on attitude change of characteristics of the communicator, the communication, and the person to whom the communication is addressed. Much has been learned from these studies; an illustrative finding, called the "sleeper effect," is that the influence of a low-credibility communicator, while at first seemingly rejected, may be detected after the passage of a few weeks' time.

Other psychologists have noted the common element present in get-acquainted programs of churches and other organizations, international exchange-of-persons programs, and the unintended associations experienced as a result of enforced desegregation. Each such program has the potential of bringing about personal contact with members of a disliked group. Common sense has it that getting to know people through such contacts leads to liking them. Psychologists studying attitude change know this is by no means always the case. Their research has indicated that under certain conditions attitudes of people in contact do become more favorable. Under other conditions, however, they worsen. For example, in the pattern of favorable conditions one usually finds cooperation in achieving some mutual objective; in the unfavorable pattern, by contrast, one often sees competition for scarce rewards.

The influence of personal contact on attitude change has been studied both in natural experiments and in the laboratory. The natural experiments have developed in the course of desegregation in the armed services, in industry, in education, and in housing. From studies in such settings hypotheses about attitude change gradually emerged. Then, in order to study these hypotheses under greater control, experiences duplicating those of real life were set up in laboratories where the experimenter could determine exactly what took place. From such experiments should eventually come the kind of knowledge needed to manage desegregation in such a way as to produce constructive outcomes.

Another approach to attitude change is based on the need of an individual for consistency between his attitudes and his behavior. People who engage in certain behaviors tend to develop attitudes that are consistent with or that justify these behaviors. Suppose, for example, that an individual is asked to assert and develop and espouse arguments that run counter to—and are thus inconsistent with—his own personal attitudes. The aroused feeling of tension, or inconsistency, should necessitate a change in attitude. It has been shown experimentally that this is true: persons required to prepare an argument for formal debate, then made to take the side with which they privately disagree, shift toward the position which they are asked to represent—with the shift being greater if they receive approval for their arguments. Such a phenomenon has also been observed in the much more extreme situation in which prisoners were ordered to first copy, and then compose, Communist propaganda; the resultant "brain washing" has been well documented. As a prisoner (especially when he is deprived of peer group support) the individual cannot publicly retract what he says, and thus experiences strong psychological forces to shift his beliefs.

Building Resistance to Attitude Change

One of the ways in which social psychologists have attempted to understand further the nature of the forces which act to shift a person's beliefs has been by studying ways of creating defenses against, and thus building resistance to, attitude change. It has been found that "cultural truisms"—widely shared beliefs that are seldom, if ever, questioned, such as the belief that one ought to brush one's teeth often—are extremely vulnerable to attack by counterargument, probably because they never had to be defended. Two ways have been found to produce resistance to counterarguments. The first method involves provision of support for belief. The second method, similar to biological inoculation, involves exposing the person to weakened or refuted versions of the attacking arguments. Repeated experiments have demonstrated the superiority of the latter method, even when the inoculating arguments are quite different from the arguments contained in subsequent attacks.

Obvious implications for producing resistance to propagandistic arguments of the nature of "brain washing" can be derived. For example, if individuals come from an environment in which certain beliefs (for example, the belief that democracy is the best form of government) are never questioned or critically considered, that belief will be highly vulnerable to attack. On the other hand, an open society and educational system, in which free inquiry and dissent are tolerated, will be far more likely to produce the sort of inoculated, resistant beliefs that withstand attacking propaganda. It should be noted, finally, that while it is true that many beliefs are highly vulnerable, it is equally true that others—which are highly ingrained in a culture or which serve important ego-defensive functions or both—are sometimes highly resistant to change, despite attempts to change them by credible communicators.

In attempting to understand the factors which underlie the development and change of attitudes, social psychologists have found it useful to study behavior as it occurs within a variety of social contexts. In doing so, it has been assumed that the things people come to see and feel, the risks they take, the agreements they reach with one another, and so on are strongly influenced by the behavior of those around them as well as by their environment.

Group Risk-Taking

A recent development in the study of social influence processes has concerned the level of risk which a group will accept relative to that which its individual members would profess. In "risk-taking" studies, individuals first privately indicate the lowest level of certainty they would demand before recommending a particular course of action. Subsequently a group is formed, and a problem is discussed until consensus is reached. With remarkable regularity, the level of risk agreed upon by the group is substantially higher than that reflected in the average of the individual judgments. Groups, of whatever age, sex, occupation, or nationality, tend to take greater risks than their individual members.

As the results come in from the many variations on this line of research, it becomes evident that the events critical in producing the "risky shift" occur during the process of group discussion. And it is the discussion itself—not the requirement that the group reach consensus or that they be able to see each other—that appears to be the condition responsible for producing the shift. What gets vocalized, however, is a multiplicity of things, of which only some are apparently crucial.

One plausible interpretation of the role of discussion in producing the shift is that, at least in western cultures, moderate risk-taking is positively valued. One should be "venturesome" but not "foolhardy." Group discussion may act to establish the appropriate level of "moderate riskiness" for a particular situation.

One might think that the individuals who win in arguing for high levels of risk in group discussion are personally stronger and more influential members. The research evidence, however, has not yet shown this to be an important factor. Nevertheless, the proponent of risk may gain an advantage over other group members because of the language available to him. The rhetoric of risk may be richer and more dramatic and hence more convincing. Moreover, the uncertainties entailed in accepting high risk may enable the proponent to state his arguments with heightened intensity and amplitude.

A still further possibility is that, in the course of group discussion, the group members come to feel that they share the responsibility for any negative aspects of their risk-taking, and that causality for disaster will not be attributed to any single member. This diffusion of responsibility is, in a sense, a protection from blame, which may be a stronger motive than the desire to claim credit for success.

Bargaining

The psychological processes inherent in mutual influence are highly complex, as can be seen in recent studies of interpersonal bargaining. The bargaining process proceeds smoothly as long as there is little conflict of interest between the two parties involved (that is, when each can meet the demands of the other without seriously hurting himself). In such cases, differences can be resolved by "gentlemen's agreements," simple rules are derived which lead to coordinated behavior or to equitable sharing or both, and there is little evidence of distrust or deceitfulness. The relationship changes dramatically, however, as the conflict of interest between the two parties increases, as the demands of each can be satisfied only by hurting the other. Informal agreements that might control the conflict are now very difficult to reach since proposals from either side to negotiate the dispute are subject to distrust and misinterpretation by the other. The stronger party is tempted to exploit the weaker one, who in turn is tempted to withdraw completely from the bargaining relationship.

There appear, however, to be some conditions under which formal contractual agreements to control conflict can be reached. Current research indicates that these contractual agreements are likely to occur in the presence of both a disinterested third party having no conflict of interest with either of the disputants and an increase in the attractiveness of the weaker party's external opportunities, thus giving greater credibility to his threat to withdraw from the negotiation. Under these conditions there appears to be a good chance of reaching a formal agreement in which each party, in return for protection from the other, is required to inhibit its power to damage and disrupt.

Clearly bargaining research has implications for certain domestic problems (for example, labor-management disputes) as well as for international disputes, negotiations, and agreements. An issue which is only beginning to be explored is that concerned with the "control" over people in high power positions exercised by those whose power would ordinarily be reckoned as smaller (as in student and faculty disputes or in warfare between small and large nations).

International Psychology

Most of the discoveries concerning attitudes, social influence, and group behavior have resulted from studies of individuals from the mainstream of North American and European societies. Until recently, the great majority of work dealing with human development, personality, and social psychology was based upon English-speaking, middle-class children and young adults who were readily accessible in schools, colleges, and the military services. Severely limited resources for research, coupled with the convenience of interesting problems close at hand, meant that most investigators chose to study social psychological problems within their own institutions and societies, frequently using samples of volunteers drawn from the classroom. As a result, generalizations based upon many of the substantive findings from this work must be limited to a relatively narrow band of sociocultural variation.

A new kind of comparative study has emerged in the past fifteen years, a cross-cultural psychology which looks for diversity across nations, languages, and even throughout the entire universe of contemporary man. A natural extension of ethnopsychological research done largely by anthropologists on culture and personality, this new development is the result of the rapid growth of international psychology, the availability of more powerful concepts, measuring instruments, and methods of data analysis, and the increased support for social research in general.

The study of cultural factors in human behavior requires a search for enough variation in style of life, language, educational practice, belief systems, values, the handling of aggression, achievement, and many other characteristics to provide the contrasts needed for comparative analysis. But the more diversity of this type that is present, the greater the difficulty of employing relevant measurement techniques that have a standardized meaning. A test, scale, or experimental technique that might be appropriate for an educated western culture may not work at all for an African tribesman or Indian villager. The introduction of cross-national, cross-language, and subcultural factors in the study of human behavior enormously complicates the research plan. Yet without such a broadened scope, important questions vital to our understanding of the sociocultural determinants of human development and behavior remain unanswered.

A solid basis for comparative psychological studies in different societies must be established before rigorous cross-cultural research can be undertaken. The cross-cultural standardization of techniques for collecting and interpreting psychological data usually requires competent co-investigators who are thoroughly familiar with each culture under consideration. Ideally, this competence can best be achieved by an international group of native co-investigators who work together on an equal basis, each claiming a special competence by virtue of his national, linguistic, and cultural identification. A major deterrent to the development of international psychology is the uneven growth of research competence and facilities across different countries. Another interfering factor has been the confusion between behaviorial research in foreign countries and its presumed relation to intelligence activities. True scientific investigation should never be confused with other operational activities. Psychologists as members of a scientific community must be on guard against having their efforts misinterpreted, both by members of the overseas scientific community and by the U.S. military and political authorities. True science should be in the interest of all and should not simply serve narrow nationalistic concerns.

10
THE NUMBERS OF PSYCHOLOGISTS

Psychology is both a science and a profession. When most people think of psychology, they imagine the professional at work in the clinics, in hospitals, in the counselor's office, or as a consultant to management in business or education. This picture represents the part of psychology that becomes involved in the world's work, helping people, enriching education and training, developing tests and measures, improving management, and otherwise becoming enmeshed in the day-to-day activities of a modern industrial society. Behind and at the base of this service structure lies the academy, with its programs of scientific study, education, and training.

To estimate the number of psychological scientists poses a problem, for in psychology no orderly sorting out of persons on professional and academic dimensions is possible. Even within graduate departments, faculty members will often have mixed orientations. And in professional practice, many psychologists devote a substantial portion of their time and effort to research.

The American Psychological Association (APA) is the central organization of psychologists in America, admitting to membership psychologists with either a professional or scientific orientation. Its membership in 1969 was 28,827. The growth in size of APA since 1945 is shown in Table 10-1. In an interval when the adult population in the United States increased by about 50 percent, APA increased in membership by almost 600 percent.

106

APA membership underestimates the number of employed psychologists. Surveys of psychologists in several metropolitan areas have found about 1.5 qualified persons employed in work of a psychological nature for every APA member, suggesting that today

TABLE 10–1   GROWTH OF THE AMERICAN PSYCHOLOGICAL ASSOCIATION

Year	Number of Members
1945	4,173
1950	7,273
1955	13,475
1960	18,215
1965	23,561
1969	28,827

Source: American Psychological Association

the United States uses 75,000 psychologists in one job or another. The modal degree held by these persons is the MA in psychology.

The great diversity of their loci of employment and the varieties of activities they pursue increases the difficulty of estimating the total number of psychologists. This may not have been entirely apparent in the earlier chapters of this report, which emphasized the scientific contributions of psychologists rather than the wide variety of their service roles. A significant number of psychologists work in hospitals, schools, industrial settings, and military establishments as active participants in the work of those agencies. Many of these persons do not hold a doctoral degree and may carry occupational titles other than that of psychologist. Table 10–2 provides evidence of this diversity of employment, even though the limitations of the data lead to an understatement of the employment of psychologists outside of universities.

Another view of the varieties of psychologists may be obtained by noting the membership of the various divisions of the American Psychological Association. The data in Table 10–3 underscore the service rather than science orientation of a large number of its members. These memberships overlap because it is possible to join more than one division. If divisional membership is representative of all psychology, then clearly most psychologists are strongly oriented toward helping individuals and society since the membership is much

TABLE 10–2 DISTRIBUTION OF PSYCHOLOGISTS BY EMPLOYMENT SETTING, 1968

Type of Employer	Total Psychologists	With PhD	With MA	Other Psychologists
Educational institution	12,810	8,658	4,039	173
Nonprofit	2,318	1,410	870	38
Industry and business	1,747	1,001	716	30
Other	176	90	83	3
Self-employed	1,402	1,084	300	18
Federal government	1,443	1,069	360	14
Other government	1,977	916	1,022	39
Military	256	142	109	5
Total	22,129	14,370	7,499	260

Source: National Science Foundation, *American Science Manpower*, 1968, Appendix Table A–5 (in press).

Note: These data tend to over-represent those persons employed as psychologists who are easily accessible, either as members of APA or as employees of universities and well-established laboratories, and to under-represent practitioners and persons without the PhD degree.

smaller for those who identify themselves in a subject matter domain such as experimental psychology and physiological psychology.

This observation is relevant to the examination of the size of psychology in comparison to the other behavioral and social sciences. Psychology outnumbers the other disciplines. It does so, mainly, because it combines academic subject matter with techniques and knowledge that are applicable to various problem areas. These applications occur in a variety of settings: in clinics, training centers, mental hospitals, manufacturing plants, and business offices. The usefulness of this work is attested, to some degree at least, by the increasing demand for qualified persons to provide the service. The response to the demand has led to the rapid growth in numbers of

TABLE 10–3 MEMBERSHIP IN DIVISIONS OF APA (1968)

Work with Individuals		
Clinical psychology	3,398	
Counseling psychology	1,735	
Psychotherapy	1,077	
Psychological aspects of disability	1,022	
		7,232
Work with Institutions		
Educational psychology	2,856	
School psychologists	1,228	
Industrial psychology	1,042	
Psychologists in public service	628	
Consulting psychology	593	
Society of engineering psychologists	407	
Military psychology	383	
Consumer psychology	281	
		7,418
Social Development and Social Psychology		
Personality and social psychology	4,168	
Society for the psychological study of social issues	1,610	
Developmental psychology	861	
Community psychology	622	
Maturity and old age	313	
		7,574
Laboratory and Quantitative Psychology		
Experimental psychology	1,074	
Evaluation and measurement	843	
Experimental analysis of behavior	623	
Physiological and comparative psychology	519	
Behavioral pharmacology	373	
		3,432
Other		
Teaching of psychology	2,302	
General psychology	1,252	
Philosophical psychology	535	
History of psychology	312	
Psychology and the arts	288	
		4,689
Total		30,345

Source: American Psychological Association

Note: Membership in the divisions of APA exceeds actual total 1968 membership of 27,250 since members may belong to more than one division.

psychologists. Without such demand, and the accompanying support for education, training, faculty positions, and research studies, the numbers of psychologists would have grown since 1945 at a much slower rate.

11

SUPPORT FOR PSYCHOLOGICAL RESEARCH

The psychologists with whom we are primarily concerned in this report are those who contribute to the science of psychology by conducting research and reporting their findings. The size of this central core of psychological work has increased substantially during the past twenty years and has received increasing support.

Federal obligations for research in psychology, in relation to the totals for all of the behavioral and social sciences, are presented in Figure 11–1 for the period 1959 to 1969. Table 11–1 relates the same data to federal support of all science and to support for the behavioral and social sciences. The support for psychology represents a substantial part of the total support for all of the behavioral and social sciences, but this proportion has been diminishing, from 53 percent in 1961 to 36 percent in 1967, particularly as the support for sociology, anthropology, and political science has increased from virtually nothing. Table 11–2 shows the overall support for psychology from federal sources, broken down by agencies awarding the funds for fiscal year 1968.

Psychology receives only a small portion of the total federal funds for research and development (approximately 1 percent in 1967). A large share of the funds for psychology aids in the support of programs directly related to mental health and comes from the National Institute of Mental Health. Other funds support programs that cut across a wide variety of disciplines. In these tabulations, money that is counted as supporting psychology may cover work by persons in other disciplines. However, it is also possible that some

111

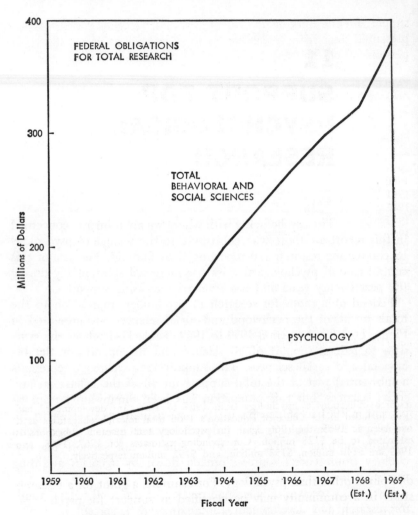

FIGURE 11–1   FEDERAL OBLIGATIONS FOR BEHAVIORAL AND SOCIAL SCIENCE RESEARCH

Source: National Science Foundation, *Federal Funds for Research, Development, and Other Scientific Activities, Fiscal Years 1967, 1968, and 1969*, Vol. 17, NSF 68–27, 1968, p. 230.

support for the work of psychologists is omitted from the summaries presented since many psychologists work in settings administered by persons other than psychologists to whom funds are granted for

TABLE 11–1   FEDERAL OBLIGATIONS FOR TOTAL RESEARCH, BASIC AND APPLIED, IN MILLIONS OF DOLLARS

Fiscal Year	All Fields of Science	All Behavioral and Social Science	Psychology
1959	$1403	$55	$24
1960	1941	73	38
1961	2620	96	51
1962	3273	120	57
1963	4041	152	72
1964	4464	197	95
1965	4854	230	103
1966	5271	266	100
1967	5273	297	108
1968 (est.)	5406	321	113
1969 (est.)	5990	382	131

Source: National Science Foundation, *Federal Funds for Research, Development, and Other Scientific Activities, Fiscal Years 1967, 1968, and 1969*, Vol. 17, NSF 68–27, 1968, p. 230.

Note: Starting in 1966, the Office of Education began assigning a portion of its total research and development obligations to "development," whereas previously it had not done so. This accounts for the apparent drop in total research obligations to psychology from 1965 to 1966. If "development" had been included in the Office of Education's 1966 total research obligations as it had been in 1965, the 1966 figure for psychology total research obligations is estimated to be $128 million. Corresponding estimates for 1967, 1968, and 1969 are $140 million, $153 million, and $192 million respectively.

disciplines other than psychology. For example, a grant for a research study in a community may be classified as support for psychology, or for psychiatric research, or for sociology, or in some other way that is not included as support for psychology. The research team in that setting might include psychiatrists, pediatricians, psychologists, sociologists, economists, linguists, statisticians, and so on.

No small part of the support for psychology has come from agencies concerned with both science and service. At the end of World

**TABLE 11–2   FEDERAL OBLIGATIONS FOR RESEARCH IN PSYCHOLOG-
ICAL SCIENCES BY AGENCY, FISCAL YEAR 1968 (ESTIMATED), IN THOU-
SANDS OF DOLLARS**

	Biological	Social	Total
Department of Commerce			
Bureau of the Census	....	$485	$485
Department of Defense			
Department of the Army	$5,316	2,676	7,992
Department of the Navy	1,127	6,273	7,400
Department of the Air Force	6,286	566	6,852
Defense agencies	310	992	1,302
Department-wide funds	96	554	650
Department of Health, Education, and Welfare			
Food and Drug Administration	....	152	152
Office of Education	....	17,812	17,812
Public Health Service	26,589	23,222	49,811
[National Institute of Mental Health]	[18,450]	[17,529]	[35,979]
[National Institutes of Health]	[8,139]	[5,693]	[13,832]
Social and Rehabilitation Service	....	2,788	2,788
Department of the Interior			
Bureau of Commercial Fisheries	526	....	526
Other Agencies			
Civil Service Commission	....	146	146
National Aeronautics & Space Administration	4,742	....	4,742
National Science Foundation	5,416	2,598	8,014
Peace Corps	....	153	153
Veterans Administration	3,583	337	3,920
Office of Science and Technology	4	4	8
Total: all agencies	53,995	58,758	112,753

Source: National Science Foundation, *Federal Funds for Research, Development,
and Other Scientific Activities, Fiscal Years 1967, 1968, and 1969,* Vol. 17, NSF
68–27, 1968, p. 147.

Note: All Department of Labor funds are officially allocated to economic research, although a review of their list of grants and contracts suggests that psychological research is also supported.

War II the Veterans Administration was faced with the serious problem of handling large numbers of persons diagnosed as having neuropsychiatric disorders. It was faced also with the problem of providing adequate occupational and educational counseling for the large number of persons returning from military service in World War II. An imaginative program of support for psychological training, which included the Veterans Administration's employing the trainees, enabled that agency to meet its needs effectively and, at the same time, to help enlarge the group of psychologists able to deal with problems of this sort. There was no blueprint for finding the necessary manpower to deal with these critical problems. It was out of the question to expect that enough psychiatrists would be prepared in short order to handle the tremendous number of cases involved. The Veterans Administration wisely foresaw the great attractiveness of clinical psychology to large numbers of able undergraduate students and provided a means of attracting them into the field and of supporting their training.

The National Institute of Mental Health (NIMH) has developed an equally imaginative program. In the examination of behavior disorders the psychologist is the best equipped member of the research team. As research programs supported by the NIMH have increased, the number of psychologists in those programs has also increased. The research programs of NIMH were more oriented towards problems than toward a learned discipline. As an important consequence, research in problems of mental health has included not merely psychiatrists and psychologists but all of the behavioral and social sciences and many biologically and mathematically oriented disciplines. Research is directed primarily towards specific problems, often involving teams which cut across disciplinary lines. Excellent procedures that emphasize the association of persons from various disciplines have been developed for the review of proposals.

The early work of the Office of Naval Research (ONR), later augmented and to a substantial degree supplanted by the National Science Foundation, provided assistance for basic and applied research in psychology. This assistance came at a critical period when opportunities for research in psychology appeared extremely attractive to prospective applicants and when large numbers of undergraduate students were moving into graduate study and required support. Much of the credit for the vigor and quality of psychological research, and for the advanced state of knowledge in some areas of psychology, is due to the research support provided by ONR during these crucial times.

In recent years a similar impact on psychology has resulted from the development of regional centers for educational research, the establishment of programs for the study of learning in the preschool period by the Office of Education, and the creation of various programs in the Office of Educational Opportunity. One effect of this work is to produce a marked increase in interest in educational psychology and in the number of persons who are working on problems of educating human beings in a natural setting. The need for this increased effort has been clear for years; the provision of research support to attract persons into the field and to provide them with the facilities they need for doing good work is critical.

The National Institute of Mental Health (NIMH) acted wisely in providing funds to be used for basic research at the same time that they supported a substantial amount of work directly related to their mission. The basic research has paid off handsomely in providing better understanding of many aspects of mental health and illness. NIMH has also supported the education of additional workers who have dealt more directly with applied problems. Similar provisions will be equally essential as other agencies begin to provide support for psychology. The attractiveness of supporting work directly related to one's mission is obvious. The need for blending that research into a larger matrix of psychological science, with less necessity for proving its immediate practical merit, is essential, however, if progress is to be made towards improving our knowledge of many aspects of human behavior. This point has been stressed repeatedly by illustrations in the earlier sections of this report.

The picture of financial support for psychological research cannot be drawn in full detail because every employer of psychologists supports directly or indirectly some form of psychological research. This is true even when the job expectation is primarily one of service rather than research. Unlike research in other sciences, psychological research is directly and actively related to problem solving; it does not have as its basis a body of abstract knowledge from which the research results. Thus a great deal of support for psychological research is provided by universities, by business, and by industrial concerns. A substantial amount of research is done in the federal government by psychologists who are not employed specifically in research and development. Direct federal support for research in psychology is the increment which makes possible effective action on a whole class of problems, action that in turn has an accelerating effect on less obvious forms of research.

CURRENT STATUS OF FEDERAL SUPPORT FOR PSYCHOLOGY

The following summary of current major sources of federal research support is condensed from a report prepared by the Board of Scientific Affairs of the American Psychological Association.

National Science Foundation (NSF)

NSF supports research in psychology through grants made by the Division of Social Sciences and the Psychobiology Program of the Division of Biological and Medical Sciences. Appropriations for fiscal year 1968 were estimated at $8.9 million dollars for the two programs combined. NSF traineeships and fellowships are made directly to universities, and NSF does not determine how these funds are distributed among science departments. Psychologists (except clinical) are supported by NSF's traineeship and fellowship programs.

National Institute of Mental Health (NIMH)

This institute, which since January 1, 1967, has been an independent bureau within the Public Health Service, provides financial support to psychologists through the following programs: Extramural Research, Manpower and Training, and Mental Health Service Programs. NIMH also supports facility grants.

National Institute of Child Health and Human Development (NICHD)

Maternal health, child health, and human development are the areas in which NICHD supports research and training. Its interests are in processes of growth and development from the prenatal stage to old age. NICHD also provides funds for assisting in construction costs of centers for research on mental retardation.

National Institute of Neurological Diseases and Stroke, and the National Eye Institute

These are now separate institutes; the activities of both were formerly under a single institute of Neurological Diseases and Blindness. NINDS provides funds for research and training in the neurological and related fields. Of special interest to psychologists is its program of support for training and research in sensory physiology as well as in audiology and speech pathology. This institute supports research concerned with the cause, development, therapy, and prevention of aphasia, mental retardation, and other disorders of the nervous system, hearing, and speech. The National Eye Institute is concerned with problems relating to vision.

Office of Education (OE)

The Office of Education supports specific projects as well as broad programs. Projects may be in any area of research related to education from development of curriculum materials to theoretical formulations in the behavioral sciences. Program support is for the development of long-term and continuous research activities, often in the form of research and development centers.

Department of Defense

Some agencies of this department support psychological research through grants and contracts. The two agencies directly supporting the behavioral and social sciences are the Office of Naval Research and the Division of Behavioral Sciences of the Advanced Research Projects Agency.

National Aeronautics and Space Administration (NASA)

NASA supports basic and applied research in several areas of psychology which are considered space-related: human engineering, sensory processes, and central nervous system functioning. It provides training grants for pre- and postdoctoral students in space-related science and technology.

Social and Rehabilitation Service of HEW

The Social and Rehabilitation Service of HEW provides funds for several extramural programs in the behavioral sciences. Among their programs of interest to psychologists are their Research and Demonstration Grants, Research and Training Center Grants, and their Demonstration Projects (with major emphasis centered on improving treatment, training and rehabilitation programs for the severely retarded and multiple handicapped residents living within the institution). The Service also provides some support for postdoctoral and special fellowships.

12

PSYCHOLOGY AND THE UNIVERSITIES

Less than 40 percent of all psychologists are employed in colleges and universities; the percentage who are members of departments awarding the PhD is much smaller. Yet this segment of psychologists is critical for the future of psychology since they train those who will become contributors to psychology and those who will apply psychological findings to human problems.

One hundred and twenty departments of psychology in the United States awarded PhD degrees during the interval 1960 to 1966. To get information on the amount of support for training psychologists and for psychologists' research activities, a questionnaire was sent to these departments in 1968. Replies were received from 108 departments (see the Appendix). (Further information concerning this questionnaire survey is provided in the appendix to the general report of the Central Planning Committee, *The Behavioral and Social Sciences: Outlook and Needs.*) Their responses provide an estimate of the level and changing nature of the activity of these departments. They represent, perhaps, the best view of the changing nature of the field and the ways in which funds are now used and will be needed in the future.

An examination of support for research in departments that award the doctoral degree provides a distorted picture of the field as a whole, for at least 530 departments in colleges or universities offer degree work in psychology but do not award a PhD degree. Although the sample of 108 (of 120) departments places some limitations on the survey findings, these 108 departments were in the universities that received 78 percent of federal funds for all areas of academic science in 1963.

The PhD-granting departments are important because they will take the lead in proposals to innovate and retool as the discipline of

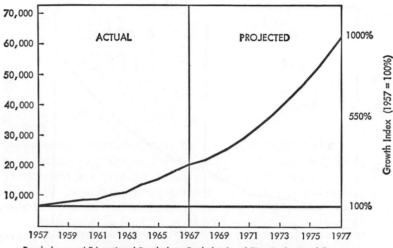

Psychology and Educational Psychology Bachelors' and First Professional Degrees Actually Awarded, 1957 – 1967, and Projected to 1977

FIGURE 12–1   NUMBER OF BACHELOR'S DEGREES AWARDED

Source: Office of Education, for 1957–1967 Degrees; *The Behavioral and Social Sciences: Outlook and Needs* (Englewood Cliffs, New Jersey: Prentice-Hall, 1969), Appendix D, for projections 1968–1977.

psychology evolves. They will train the teachers of future generations of clinicians and researchers. These are places where much of the new knowledge is discovered and from them the greatest influences on the field will emanate. These institutions provide faculty members and staff for the colleges and universities that do not award the doctoral degree, and for research in government, in non-profit research centers, and in industry. The leadership of these departments commends them to our particular attention as we try to estimate how the field will grow for the next ten years or so.

These departments also reflect most sensitively the nature of the changes in psychology in the past several years. Figures 12–1, 12–2, and 12–3 portray the growth in numbers of bachelor's, master's, and doctoral degrees awarded in psychology since 1957 and project the estimates of numbers of these degrees to be produced each year up

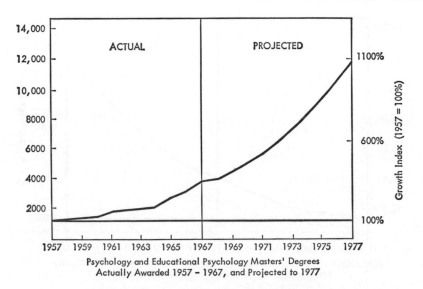

Psychology and Educational Psychology Masters' Degrees
Actually Awarded 1957 – 1967, and Projected to 1977

FIGURE 12–2   NUMBER OF MASTER'S DEGREES AWARDED

Source: Office of Education, for 1957–1967 degrees; *The Behavioral and Social Sciences: Outlook and Needs* (Englewood Cliffs, New Jersey: Prentice-Hall, 1969), Appendix D, for projections 1968–1977.

to 1977. (Detailed information on the methods of projection will be found in the appendix to the survey committee's general report, *The Behavioral and Social Sciences: Outlook and Needs* [Englewood Cliffs, New Jersey: Prentice-Hall, 1969]). The growth rate of the last ten years is expected to continue but not to accelerate. The data indicate the necessity for departments of psychology to plan for larger faculties, increased student support, and, as a natural corollary to an expanding PhD program, increased funds for research.

An analysis of past status and of the likely needs of psychology in the near future can also be obtained by examining reports from departments of psychology on the number of faculty members, expressed in full-time equivalents, in 1962 and in 1967, and the number projected as required in 1972 and 1977. The overall estimate of future growth from our sample of departments indicates that they do not expect to grow any more rapidly in the future than they have in the past.

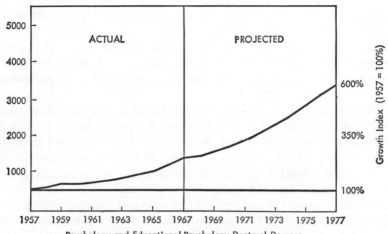

Psychology and Educational Psychology Doctoral Degrees
Actually Awarded, 1957 – 1967, and Projected to 1977

FIGURE 12–3   NUMBER OF DOCTORAL DEGREES AWARDED

Source: Office of Education, for 1957–1967 degrees; *The Behavioral and Social Sciences: Outlook and Needs* (Englewood Cliffs, New Jersey: Prentice-Hall, 1969), Appendix D, for projections 1968–1977.

However, this is not uniformly true. Departments that intend to grow most rapidly are not the ones enjoying the highest prestige at present as reported by Allan Cartter in *An Assessment of Quality in Graduate Education* (Washington, D.C.: American Council on Education, 1966). The prestigious, well-established departments tend to plan for only modest growth. Departments desiring to increase most in size are those which either are on the threshold of considerable strength, or are of recent origin (for example, in some of the large state universities), or may be of unknown quality. The inference may be drawn that the rank order of departments of psychology, both in size (including numbers of degrees awarded) and in prestige, in the next decade could change considerably.

Similar data relating to geographic regions of the country suggest that departments of psychology in the South will grow most rapidly. Only a small number of psychology departments in the southern United States were rated among the best in the country in the Cartter study. Any substantial growth in the less distinguished departments in the South without an accompanying improvement in quality could retard the development of the field of psychology as a whole. Those responsible for the distribution of funds to support research, graduate training, and departmental development must recognize this possibility and encourage qualitative improvement there as well as growth.

The figures and charts presented in the preceding chapter obscure the great complexity of financial support for psychology. Any department of psychology finds that its problems include management of support for graduate students, purchase of equipment, maintenance of the instructional program, and provision for the recruitment and retention of faculty. University funds are rarely adequate to meet all of the needs of the department. An able and vigorous department chairman with a good faculty can attract support for his department through training grants from the National Institute of Mental Health or the National Institutes of Health, and graduate student support through NSF traineeships, NDEA fellowships, and federal research programs.

In addition, research grants to individual faculty members can enable a department to acquire equipment that the faculty member will use not merely in his own research but also in the education and training of graduate and even undergraduate students. Such funds may also support graduate students by providing research assistantships. Moreover, the universities in the questionnaire survey sample frequently used funds from their own resources for support of research activities and recruited funds from a variety of private agencies. A number of private foundations (for examples, the Carnegie Corporation of New York and the Rockefeller Foundation) support work in psychology as part of their overall programs.

Some suggestions of the nature of this complexity are provided in

TABLE 12–1   RESEARCH EQUIPMENT AND SPACE NEEDS

Reserch Equipment	
Current replacement value, 1967	$26,366,000
Estimated costs over next 5 years, 1967–1972	$19,372,000
Estimated costs over next 10 years, 1967–1977	$34,026,000
Space Requirement	
Current space available, 1967	3,149,500 sq. ft.
Total space needed by fiscal year 1972	5,499,000 sq. ft.
Total space needed by fiscal year 1977	6,775,000 sq. ft.

Source: Departmental questionnaire to 120 PhD-granting departments. (Figures are corrected to include 12 non-respondents.)

Table 12–1. It notes the responses of departments concerning the value of their equipment and their needs for 1972 and 1977, and their space and anticipated space needs in 1972 and 1977. That new space, estimated at $55 per square foot, will cost nearly 200 million dollars over the period 1967–1977 (if building costs do not rise). Responding departments also reported annual charges for computing amounting to over a million dollars. These costs have risen geometrically in the past several years and promise to continue to rise out of all proportion to other measures of growth in psychological research.

Psychology continues to attract large numbers of able graduate students. Most of those who enroll in PhD programs obtain support during their period of graduate study. Sources of support are varied. Yet it is necessary to identify sources of support ahead of time in order to make firm offers and associated stipends to prospective graduate students at the appropriate time of the year. This matter has become a particularly acute concern during the last year or two when funds for research support have been reduced. The PhD-granting departments were able to offer financial support to 70 percent of all newly entering graduate students in the Fall of 1967. The sources of this support are shown in Table 12–2. By comparison to other social sciences, psychology is provided with relatively good support for these students; the picture is less favorable in comparison to the physical sciences, where 81 percent of newly entering students receive support (1965 data).

TABLE 12–2   FINANCIAL AID FOR NEWLY ENTERING GRADUATE STU-
DENTS, FALL TERM 1967 (PHD-GRANTING PSYCHOLOGY DEPARTMENTS)

Type and Source	Number of Students Assisted	Percentage Assisted	Total Annual Assistance	Average Stipend
Scholarships/Fellowships				
Woodrow Wilson	24	1		
NSF	55	2		
Public Health Service (NIH and NIMH)	91	3		
National Defense Education Act (NDEA and NDFL)	249	9		
University Scholarships/ Fellowships	205	7		
Other Scholarships/ Fellowships	69	2		
[Subtotal]	[693]	[24]	$2,189,600	$3200
Traineeship Grants				
Public Health Service (NIH and NIMH)	566	20		
NSF	113	4		
Other Traineeship Grants	197	7		
[Subtotal]	[876]	[31]	$2,721,600	$3100
Assistantships				
Teaching or Lab Assistant	648	23		
Research Assistantships	470	17		
Readerships or Other	49	2		
[Subtotal]	[1167]	[42]	$3,166,500	$2700
Other Financial Assistance	77	3		
[Subtotal]	[77]	[3]	$ 180,000	$2300
Total	2813	100	$8,257,700	$2900

Source: Departmental Questionnaire.

The domains of study in psychology require each department to have a much greater variety of physical resources at its disposal than might otherwise be necessary. The equipment in a department of psychology often includes surgical apparatus, particularly for work with animals; telemetering services; electrophysiological equipment; acoustical chambers; computer monitored systems, to provide careful sensory control and precise recording of responses; experimental rooms for study of perceptual process or of social interactions; optical benches; multichannel recorders; and on-line computers.

Almost every department requires facilities for a variety of animals. Although rats are most commonly used, mice, monkeys, pigeons, and dogs are also used frequently; some experimenters work with fish, earthworms, dolphins, bats, ducks, pigs, or the planarian, a freshwater flatworm. Many investigators study human verbal responses, using tape recorders, multichannel recorders, and elaborate control devices. Others work with different forms of human behavior and may require memory drums, tachistoscopes, pursuit rotors, and similar devices. Social psychologists may use elaborate facilities for small group experiments and observation. They may also require facilities for the collection of survey data and tabulating and computing resources for their analyses. Some will conduct studies in an experimental school, in a clinic, a hospital, or a nursery, and they may have laboratories built into trailers so that they can visit these settings. They may require closed circuit TV for the recording of material observed, or cameras, projectors, and other similar equipment. Those studying problems in reading may have eye movement cameras. Almost every department will have some form of shop, either for woodworking or for electronics. Many will require photographic darkrooms.

This description of psychology reflects the almost total departure of the field from the simple "armchair" procedures that were common in the early part of the century. Those have been replaced by carefully controlled studies of many aspects of the organism. Small wonder that the department itself has become a far more complex organization. It becomes involved not only in teaching undergraduates, who ought to know something about principles of human behavior, but also in training undergraduates as preprofessionals, who are learning something about the complex techniques of psychology.

It also has a substantial number of graduate students working on research activities closely related to those of the faculty members. The faculty members themselves conduct elaborate research programs. A large department may employ a business manager, a crew of technical workers, a caretaker for the animal laboratory; it may also operate one or more workshops. These requirements of a complex department of psychology place a great burden on the institution supporting it.

To describe psychology in the university without calling attention to its relation with other programs of instruction would provide an inadequate picture of the field. Almost every department of psychiatry includes a substantial number of psychologists, and increasing numbers of psychologists are to be found in other departments of medical schools. Psychologists are also integrally involved in colleges of education, business administration, and journalism. Frequently on the university campus psychologists will work in a department of home economics or a department or institute of child development. They also serve in institutes of industrial relations, in law schools, in schools of social work, in programs of physical medicine, in counseling services, and in health service on the campus. They may be in the department of pediatrics in the medical school or in the college of engineering, particularly those concerned with man-machine relationships and operations research. Psychologists may also be involved in research activities associated with the university as a whole either in programs of institutional research or studies in higher education, or in research having to do with the quality of instruction or the evaluation of faculty.

The general report, *The Behavioral and Social Sciences: Outlook and Needs*, records the total number of behavioral and social scientists in professional schools located at PhD-granting universities. In the survey of 447 professional schools within PhD-granting universities they found some 5,000 behavioral and social scientists employed in teaching or research capacities. The largest employers of behavioral and social scientists were medical schools. Next were schools of business, with education following closely behind. For psychology alone the distribution is somewhat different, as Table 12–3 shows. Psychology is most significantly represented in colleges of education, and next in colleges of medicine. Of the nearly 5,000

TABLE 12–3 PSYCHOLOGISTS EMPLOYED IN SURVEYED PROFESSIONAL SCHOOLS (1966)

Professional School	Number of Psychologists
Education	832
Medicine	544
Business	122
Public health	65
Social work	21
Public administration	2
Total	1586

Source: *The Behavioral and Social Sciences: Outlook and Needs* (Englewood Cliffs, N.J., Prentice-Hall, 1969), Table 11–1: Professional School Questionnaire.

persons identified as behavioral and social scientists cmploycd in professional schools, one-third were psychologists.

As noted earlier, 120 departments of psychology in the United States have awarded the PhD degree in psychology. However, an additional 155 or more departments of psychology around the country offer work leading to a master's degree. This number will include several departments within the same university such as educational psychology or child psychology, and many departments in those colleges and universities which do not have a doctoral program.

The expansion of PhD-granting departments includes growth not only in number of faculty but also in numbers of graduate students and in support for research undertaken by psychologists. One might ask whether it is reasonable to assume that the anticipated increases in the numbers of graduate students in psychology is likely to be realized. Are qualified applicants likely to be available?

A survey of 243 MA- and PhD-granting departments of psychology was conducted in the fall of 1968 by the American Psychological Association. Departments reported a total of 13,760 students applying for admission to graduate work in psychology. This population of applicants produced a total of 33,000 applications.

The following summary figures indicate what happened to these applicants: 6,058 (44 percent) were admitted somewhere. Of these,

2,782 submitted only one application, and were admitted; 3,161 (23 percent) of the individuals were offered some financial assistance or stipend to aid them in graduate work; 3,968 (29 percent) of the individuals applied to at least one of the 23 psychology departments ranked highest in the Cartter Report.

These data suggest that a large number of persons who apply for graduate work in psychology are not being admitted. It is not clear how many of these are qualified for graduate work. Reports from universities around the country indicate, however, that a large number of applicants for admission were rejected even though the departments considered them to be fully qualified for graduate work in that department. It is not uncommon for a department to report more than twenty-five times as many applications were received as the department could handle within its resources of space, faculty size, and facilities for research.

The attraction of psychology as a field for graduate study may be a result of the opportunities to deal with man's problems and to understand his nature from any one of a variety of vantage points. A psychologist may occupy his working time similarly to that of a neurologist, a linguist, a design engineer, an ophthalmologist, or a hospital, school, or government administrator. To each role he can bring a richness of understanding and technique by virtue of his psychological training.

13

RECOMMENDATIONS

Our committee endorses the recommendations made in the general report of this survey, *The Behavioral and Social Sciences: Outlook and Needs*. Those recommendations are not repeated here. The additional recommendations which are included in the foregoing text either augment or explicate specific issues in psychology not covered in that report.

It has been stated that to generate the new knowledge needed for imaginative and effective social programming, a large pool of trained workers is essential; many of these will be psychologists. Doubtless, many psychologists exist who could work on these problems. Whether they would be willing or whether those most able could be induced to do so is uncertain. However, sufficient challenge and support should be offered to attract the most accomplished psychologists if progress in these areas is to be realized.

RECOMMENDATION

The panel recommends that psychologists continue to gather information on behavioral processes, to integrate that information into scientific theories, and to relate those theories to practical matters of personal and social importance.

Because dealing successfully with various forms of human conduct, whether they are socially useful or undesirable, requires knowl-

131

edge of the principles of human behavior, education for all those who will deal with human behavior must be expanded and improved. For those persons who want to specialize in programs of action relating to the problems of society the educational means should be made readily available. Accordingly we propose the establishment of a new institution to assist in achieving these goals. This recommendation is identical in form to one of the major proposals in the general survey, *The Behavioral and Social Sciences: Outlook and Needs.* It is restated here because it applies exactly to the conclusion drawn by our committee.

RECOMMENDATION

The committee recommends that universities consider the establishment of broadly based training and research programs in the form of a Graduate School of Applied Behavioral Science (or some local equivalent) under administrative arrangements that lie outside the established disciplines. Such training and research should be multidisciplinary (going beyond the behavioral and social sciences as necessary), and the school should accept a responsibility for contributing through its research both to a basic understanding of human relationships and behavior and the solution of persistent social problems.

The increase in knowledge of human behavior is slow. When large numbers of persons work independently, each adding tiny increments to knowledge, the state of knowledge advances at a pace barely adequate to our need to know. The investigator who proposes a project for support which he knows will add that tiny increment to knowledge feels a reasonable expectation of gaining support for his work. In the normal course of events, research supported on a project basis guarantees an advance in knowledge. However, it may also assure that the amount of progress will be small. Every study panel reviewing proposals for project support faces the problem of balancing the quality and precision of the research against the magnitude of its possible contribution. We laud past methods for deciding which projects to support since these methods have had a profound and favorable influence in maintaining quality in psychological investigations. At the same time we recognize the need for other ways of supporting research activities in order to provide opportunities for innovation and investigation which may be much less likely to provide a payoff, but whose usefulness, if payoff is obtained, would be very great indeed. Therefore, dramatic and decisive programs of support must be established which are designed to maintain flexibility and avoid rigid formalism. The planning, operational and evaluation phases of programs must all be considered as vitally important. Also psychologists and other behavioral scientists already engaged in community improvement projects should be more amply supported not merely in their service roles, but more adequately in their research activities to insure the availability of current information about existing problems.

RECOMMENDATION

The panel recommends that the project method of support be continued in the federal agencies now using that method, with the level of support increased at between 12 and 18 percent annually over the next decade, the rate proposed in Chapter 14 of the general report, The Behavioral and Social Sciences: Outlook and Needs.

RECOMMENDATION

The panel recommends further, that psychologists increase their research on problems related to social action programs and "field experiments" that may provide insights into principles of human behavior that are difficult to study in any other way.

Psychology differs from other behavioral sciences since research support is considerably greater per capita than it is for investigators in the other behavioral sciences. The support for psychology has enabled it to progress and to contribute vigorously to the solution of human problems in a number of areas. The imaginative development of new programs in the Veterans Administration and the National Institute of Mental Health at the end of World War II prevented a serious problem by providing care and treatment of mental patients, and in the management of mental hospitals, but also more importantly in the training of new persons with a strong research orientation to work on these problems. Development in the scientific domain enabled augmentation in areas of practice and application. In common with the other social sciences, psychology needs to be adequately supported in the maintenance of its basic scientific endeavors from which these applications may develop. This is a critical issue if psychology is to provide aid in handling a wide variety of current problems.

Psychology in those areas closely allied to political science and sociology must be strengthened. We recommend strengthening the National Science Foundation in its support for basic science and psychology, and we look forward enthusiastically to its broadened charter which will provide increased support in additional areas of social science. We urge that the Foundation pursue this program vigorously and illustrate what can be accomplished as additional support is provided.

RECOMMENDATION

The panel recommends that the National Science Foundation strengthen its support of basic research in the social sciences and augment its program of support in social and political psychology.

Since psychology is a science basic to medicine, to psychiatry in particular but to other specialties as well, the National Institutes of Health have a special responsibility to see that medical students have access to satisfactory training in psychology and that these aspects of psychology that are related to medical training and practice should be scientifically as strong as possible. Although NIMH has interpreted "mental health" broadly enough to support a wide range of psychological investigations, they should not be required to bear the whole burden of supporting applications of psychology to all the other branches of medicine.

RECOMMENDATION

The panel recommends that the National Institutes of Health strengthen their support of basic research in psy-

chology, particularly in those branches of psychology that are clearly relevant to medicine and to the delivery of medical services.

Psychology has relied more and more on technical equipment for the collection and analysis of data. Sections of the report describe in detail research requiring highly sophisticated neurophysiological equipment with adequate monitoring and analytic equipment. Some forms of psychological research require the analysis of large masses of data with a variety of mathematical processes used to reduce the data to meaningful form. Many studies of language or of social or developmental behaviors require specially designed equipment to control behavior and to provide immediate, on-line reaction to the behavior emitted.

RECOMMENDATION

The panel recommends that federal agencies provide a substantial increase in support for equipment for use in psychology and in all the behavioral sciences to match technological advances in these fields. The funding for support should expand greatly the number of small and middle-sized units for monitoring and analyzing behavioral responses. These items of equipment should be made readily available for individual investigators and institutions in their own research activities.

RECOMMENDATION

The panel recommends that federal agencies provide a substantial increase in the number of small and middle-sized computers available to individual investigators and the accessibility of time on very large computers to investigators anywhere in the country.

The investigation into human behavior involves some intrusions into the private life of individuals. Generally, this intrusion is so trifling that no problem arises. In some instances the nature of the data collected or the nature of the intrusion into the life of the individual evokes questions about the value of the information collected in terms of the costs involved in the reduction of privacy. We applaud the work of the American Psychological Association in having prepared explicit statements of principle on this matter as part of their Code of Ethics. We believe, however, that the nature of privacy and the needs for privacy are often misunderstood and that psychologists are obligated to help improve understanding in this area.

RECOMMENDATION

The panel recommends that a larger number of psychologists direct their attention to the issues of privacy, both as a need of individuals, and as an attribute valued by society. They should determine the ways in which privacy and related aspects of self-esteem and individuality are related to other variables and how they affect the quality of life in a modern society. We recommend that funding agencies give support to worthy research studies on this problem.

RECOMMENDATION

The panel also recommends that public and private agencies provide support for studies of the feasibility of a social data system, to determine the best ways to safeguard privacy while providing access to basic information about our society and our human resources.

The most likely persons to resolve many of the problems which concern America are today's high school or college students who will shortly be in our graduate schools or professional schools preparing for lives of useful service. A critical problem exists in the support of graduate students, for their interests are frequently subverted by the demands placed upon them to support themselves during graduate study. The graduate student without any support has a serious problem. If he must spend his time in a research laboratory during his graduate period in order to support himself he loses the opportunity to gain adequate experience in teaching. If he supports himself essentially by teaching he loses the freedom to engage in detailed research activities that might otherwise capture his attention. We applaud the variety of federal, state, and institutional programs that permit and encourage a patterning of the activities of the student in the way that is most appropriate for his professional development. We urge that support be provided more generally so that it meets the changing needs of the student during his entire period of work towards the doctoral or professional degree.

RECOMMENDATION

The panel recommends that university and other funding agencies provide support for graduate students in psychology and in the other social sciences on a four- or five-year base with opportunities for a changing mix of activities consistent with the academic needs of the students and the educational requirements of the program in which the student is working. We believe that almost every doctoral student in psychology should spend some portion of his time in teaching under supervision and some portion of his time in research activities. Such support for graduate study should cover the modest additional costs associated with the research activities involved in the doctoral dissertation, especially if the research is concerned with a problem area requiring off-campus work.

RECOMMENDATION

The panel also recommends continued support by public and private agencies of postdoctoral education in psychology, both in areas of application in psychology, and in psychological science.

As is indicated in Chapter 12 of this report, the largest and best known graduate departments of psychology in the country are receiving applications for graduate study from many more students than they can accept or handle. These departments plan in the next decade to increase in size at approximately the same rate at which they have grown in the past ten years, while it is evident that the number of undergraduate and graduate students in the nation as a whole will increase at a much greater rate. We foresee serious dislocations and a reduction in the general quality of graduate education if these plans mature as projected. We are also concerned that the needs of society for psychological scientists and practitioners may not be met, and that students desiring to enter psychology may encounter difficulties in obtaining the education they want.

RECOMMENDATION

The panel recommends that psychologists in universities and other psychologists in the American Psychological Association review the plans of graduate departments of psychology in the light of projected growth in numbers of students, and that psychologists in association with the appropriate public and private agencies supporting graduate education in psychology take steps to assure the availability of adequate opportunities for graduate education of high quality for those able students who seek it.

EPILOGUE

This report on the field of psychology was directed at clarifying the nature of psychological study and its usefulness in improving the understanding of man and his society. We believe that psychology has demonstrated that it is worthy of support. We would be less than fully satisfied, however, if only that thesis emerged. For psychology is a fascinating field of study which can provide insights into matters that have eluded man's understanding for centuries. It is concerned with some of the most important issues of the times. It offers knowledge, techniques, and procedures useful in man's efforts to live with his fellow man and to improve the quality of life. The study of psychology increases man's humility, as he recognizes the enormous capacities of a human being and the incredibly complicated ways in which man adapts to changes in his own physiological state and in the environment in which he lives.

Today's younger generation of psychologists is a valuable asset to psychology. These bright young persons of great ingenuity have developed imaginative research studies and innovative community programs. They have been leaders in the construction of new theories and analytical techniques. We believe that, using the findings of their predecessors, many of which are outlined in this report, this younger generation will provide a substantial increment to knowledge of man, far beyond that now predictable. Therefore, it is critical that psychology be supported wisely and well—indeed, far better than might seem justified from a mere summary of its accomplishments. The

139

challenge of the future must be met in order to realize the vast potential of this field. We believe that the money already spent on psychology has been fully justified in terms of the record of its accomplishments presented in this report.

Psychology is a field that is easily susceptible to change. It has not suffered the rigidity of many other disciplines; it has accommodated itself to the changes in views and values of its members. In its early days, psychologists developed a substantial base of laboratory and experimental work that has increased the rigor and objectivity of the work of all psychologists. During the past thirty years it added an emphasis on the application of psychology to the problems of individuals. We believe that during the next generation psychology will change again. We are willing to predict that the new area of emphasis will relate to the problems of groups and societies. We not only accept this new direction but welcome it and call upon our fellow psychologists and our supporters to assist in accelerating it. As a science fitting into the total spectrum of the behavioral and social sciences, and as a profession dedicated to human welfare, psychology in this and in the next generation merits the enthusiastic support of our society.

APPENDIX

EDUCATIONAL PSYCHOLOGY DEPARTMENTS PARTICIPATING IN THE QUESTIONNAIRE SURVEY

University of Alabama
University of Arizona
Arizona State University
University of Arkansas
Boston College
Boston University
Brigham Young University*
Catholic University of America*
University of Connecticut
Emory University
Fordham University
University of Georgia
University of Hawaii
University of Illinois
Indiana University
University of Iowa
Johns Hopkins University
University of Kansas
Michigan State University
University of Minnesota

Mississippi State University
University of Nebraska
New York University*
State University of New York at
    Albany
Ohio University*
University of Oklahoma*
University of Oregon
University of the Pacific*
Pennsylvania State University
Rutgers, The State University*
University of Southern California*
Southern Illinois University
Temple University*
University of Tennessee
University of Texas, Austin
University of Utah
Washington University
Wayne State University
University of Wisconsin, Madison

* Did not respond.

PSYCHOLOGY DEPARTMENTS
PARTICIPATING IN THE QUESTIONNAIRE
SURVEY

Adelphi University[1]
University of Alabama
American University*
Adelphi University[1]
University of Alabama
University of Arizona
Arizona State University
University of Arkansas
Baylor University*
Boston College
Boston University
Brandeis University
Brigham Young University
Brown University
Bryn Mawr College
University of California, Berkeley
University of California,
    Los Angeles
University of California, Riverside
University of California, Santa
    Barbara
Carnegie-Mellon University*
Case Western Reserve University
Catholic University of America
University of Chicago[2]
University of Cincinnati
City University of New York
Claremont Graduate School
Clark University

University of Colorado
Colorado State University
Columbia University[3]
University of Connecticut
Cornell University
University of Delaware
University of Denver
Duke University
Duquesne University
Emory University
University of Florida
Florida State University
Fordham University
George Peabody College for
    Teachers
George Washington University
Georgetown University
University of Georgia
Harvard University
University of Hawaii
University of Houston
University of Illinois
Illinois Institute of Technology
Indiana University
University of Iowa
Iowa State University
Johns Hopkins University
University of Kansas
Kansas State University

[1] Two departments are included in this classification: Psychology and Institutes of Advanced Psychological Studies. (Both departments responded to the survey.)
[2] Two departments are included in this classification: Human Development and Psychology. (Both departments responded to the survey.)
[3] Two departments are included in this classification: Social Psychology responded to the survey, Psychology did not respond.

* Did not respond.

University of Kentucky
Lehigh University
Louisiana State University
University of Louisville
Loyola University*
University of Maine
University of Maryland
University of Massachusetts
Massachusetts Institute of Technology
University of Miami
University of Michigan
Michigan State University
University of Minnesota
University of Missouri at Columbia
University of Nebraska*
University of New Mexico
New School for Social Research
New York University*
State University of New York
    at Buffalo
University of North Carolina
North Carolina State University
University of North Dakota*
Northwestern University
Ohio University
Ohio State University
University of Oklahoma
Oklahoma State University
University of Oregon
University of Pennsylvania
Pennsylvania State University
University of Pittsburgh

University of Portland *
Princeton University
Purdue University*
University of Rochester
Rutgers, The State University
St. John's University
St. Louis University
University of South Carolina
University of Southern California
Southern Illinois University
University of Southern Mississippi
Stanford University
Syracuse University
Temple University*
University of Tennessee
University of Texas, Austin
Texas Christian University
Texas Technological College
Tufts University
Tulane University
University of Utah
Utah State University
Vanderbilt University
University of Virginia
University of Washington
Washington State University
Washington University
Wayne State University
West Virginia University
University of Wisconsin, Madison
University of Wisconsin,
    Milwaukee

* Did not respond.

SUGGESTED READINGS

There is a substantial body of literature in psychology available for those who want to read further. A comprehensive index of publications in psychology and closely allied fields is *Psychological Abstracts*, a periodical published by the American Psychological Association. New articles and books in psychology both in the United States and in other countries are listed by category in the individual issues of this journal. Each title is listed with a short, descriptive abstract, and each volume includes an index by subject and author.

The American Psychological Association also publishes *Contemporary Psychology*, a monthly journal containing reviews of books on psychology. The reviews are critical commentaries, and the journal attempts to review every significant new book published in the field of psychology.

Current research in various fields of psychology is reviewed in *Annual Reviews of Psychology*, published by Annual Reviews, Inc., of Palo Alto, California. A new volume of about fifteen chapters dealing with some area of psychology appears each year. Each chapter is a critical and selective review of the work published in the field since the time of the last review, usually one or two years. Excellent articles on topics in psychology are included in the seventeen volumes of the *International Encyclopedia of the Social Sciences*, published by The Macmillan Company and The Free Press in 1968.

The American Psychological Association publishes *The American Psychologist*, a monthly periodical providing information about the field of psychology. It reproduces some of the major addresses given by leaders in psychology, summarizes reports of committees and study groups, reports the dates of conventions, presents discussions of professional issues, and reports changes in positions of psychologists. The Association also publishes journals in various substantive areas of psychology such as the *Journal of Abnormal Psychology, Journal of Applied Psychology, Journal of Personality and Social Psychology,* and *Developmental Psychology.* It also publishes separate annual booklets of interest to students, such as *Graduate Study in Psychology,* which lists departments offering work toward advanced degrees and financial assistance available to graduate students. Information about these publications can be obtained by writing to the American Psychological Association, 1200 Seventeenth Street NW, Washington, D.C., 20036.

Psychological research is often reported in various media for the information of nonpsychologists. Among the best sources for such materials are *Psychology Today, Scientific American,* and *Science.* Introductory textbooks in psychology are numerous and usually well written. Guides to the best of the new texts are the reviews of them that appear in *Contemporary Psychology.*